Where Memory Dwells

Where Memory Dwells

Culture and State Violence in Chile

Macarena Gómez-Barris

UNIVERSITY OF CALIFORNIA PRESS

Berkeley   Los Angeles   London

University of California Press, one of the most distinguished university presses in
the United States, enriches lives around the world by advancing scholarship
in the humanities, social sciences, and natural sciences. Its activities are supported
by the UC Press Foundation and by philanthropic contributions from individuals
and institutions. For more information, visit www.ucpress.edu.

University of California Press
Berkeley and Los Angeles, California

University of California Press, Ltd.
London, England

Library of Congress Cataloging-in-Publication Data

Gómez-Barris, Macarena, 1970–.
  Where memory dwells : culture and state violence in Chile / Macarena
Gómez-Barris.
    p.   cm.
  Includes bibliographical references and index.
  ISBN 978-0-520-25583-8 (cloth : alk. paper) — ISBN 978-0-520-25584-5
(pbk. : alk. paper)
    1. Chile—History—1973–1988.   2. Collective memory—Chile.
3. Chile—History—1988–.   4. Art—Political aspects—Chile—History—
20th century.   I. Title.
  F3100.G653   2008
  306.20983'09047—dc22   2008008261

Manufactured in the United States of America

18 17 16 15 14 13 12 11 10 09
10 9 8 7 6 5 4 3 2 1

Chapter 3 is a revised version of "Torture Sees and Seeks: Guillermo Núñez's
Art in Chile's Transition," *A Contracorriente: A Journal of Social History and
Literature* 5, no. 1 (fall 2007): 86–107; used by permission. Parts of chapter 5
appeared as "Two 9/11s in a Lifetime: Chilean Displacement, Art, and Terror,"
Latino Studies 3, no. 1 (March 2005): 97–112; reprinted with permission of
Palgrave Macmillan.

Frontispiece: Patio 29 at the Santiago General Cemetery. Photo by Nicole Hayward.

This book is printed on Natures Book, which contains 50% post-consumer
waste and meets the minimum requirements of ANSI/NISO Z39.48-1992
(R 1997) (*Permanence of Paper*).

A los desaparecidos, los torturados, y sus familias.

To the memory of Salvador Allende Gossens

and to

Renato Emile and Amalia Ixchel,

mis hijos preciosos.

CONTENTS

ILLUSTRATIONS

ACKNOWLEDGMENTS

So many people have helped during my research and writing journey toward a return to a nation and tragedy that was formative for my family and me. Early in my endeavor, Vivianne Dufour, Arnold Bauer, Adriana Colman, Philippe De Conti, and Milena Leni each played instrumental roles in shaping my thinking about the dictatorship and its traces and remains. I am especially indebted to Roberto Leni Olivares, whose insight, partnership, and identification with the Chilean exilic world gave me permission to finally feel at home.

The University of California, Santa Cruz, provided a wonderful location from which to think about cultural matters. Rosa Linda Fregoso, Juan Poblete, Dana Takagi, John Brown Childs, Melanie Dupuis, Craig Reinarman, and Candace West are exceptional mentors. I am deeply grateful. Herman Gray has been a brilliant intellectual force and a great friend on this journey. His generous presence in my life has been nothing short of intellectually and personally sustaining. To Guillermo Delgado-P., I owe the seeds of this book, as one day during a final exam for his course "Introduction to Latino and Latin American Studies," we spent two hours scribbling notes back and forth about ideas for a project on memory, ideas he helped come to fruition. A special thanks goes to Tanya McNeill, Veronica López, Sudarat Musikawong, Barbara Barnes, Akiko Naono, and Deb Vargas, who in so many ways supported and entertained me, and always heard me out. At Santa Cruz, I also thank Pat Zavella and Olga Nájera-Ramírez, who were codirectors of the Chicano/Latino Research Center (CLRC) at the time of my dissertation fellowship there. They supported me at a crucial time. The Hemispheric Dialogues project that was led by Juan Poblete, Sonia Alvarez, Manuel Pastor, and Johnathan Fox both influenced and extended my intercontinental thinking. I extend a warm thanks to the Sociology Department at UCSC for a rich and unique sociological imagination and for material support.

In 2001 the Department of Spanish and Portuguese at the University of California, Berkeley, sponsored a one-day session on the democratic transition in Chile that proved to be decisive for this work. That day a group of poets, activists, and scholars convened, and I made many new friends, among them Raquel Olea, Soledad Bianchi, Carmen Berenger, my former mentor Jaime Concha, and Francine Masiello. My research in Chile is especially indebted to Raquel Olea, who brought me to Villa Grimaldi Peace Park for the first time. She also generously opened her home to me on more than one occasion. Guillermo Núñez's example has made me a stronger and, I hope, more visionary human being. Soledad Bianchi is a gracious soul and I greatly appreciate her vitality, intellect, and affect. During my archival research at the Fundación de Documentación y Archivo de la Vicaría de la Solidaridad, Don Hugo Montero was patient with my endless questions and search for materials. I thank him and the staff for their amazing work and vision through many decades. Olga Grau invited me to participate in her graduate seminar on memory, which gave me fresh insight into the perils of mapping memory. Kemy Oyarzún provided me with the opportunity to find gems in the film and video archives of the Department of Culture and Gender at the University of Chile. I'd also like to thank Silvio Caiozzi, Viviana Díaz, María Angélica Illanes, Carmen Luz Parot, Eugenio Ahumada, Carmen Vivanco, Mireya García, Nacho Agüero, Juan Carlos Molina, Lotty Rosenfeld, Carmen Waugh, the Fundación Salvador Allende, the Villa Grimaldi Peace Park staff, and the Agrupación de Familiares de Detenidos Desaparecidos for all they've contributed toward the completion of this project.

I am grateful to Pedro de Matta (fig. 4), Miguel Lawner (figs. 5–6), Guillermo Núñez (figs. 11–18), and Guillermo Prado (fig. 20) for permission to reproduce their work. Nicole Hayward took most of the photographs for this book in Chile, images she showed in San Francisco in September 2003. I can't thank her enough for her photography, and for our conversations and adventures together. I'd also like to thank my dear friends and members of the 9/11 Collective: Nicole Hayward, Gabriela Cabezas-Fischer, Axel Herrera, Álvaro Lagos, Roberto Leni Olivares, Mabel Negrete, Pancho Pescador (Franz Fischer), Ariel López, and Rafasz (Rafael Sanhueza). Through our organization of an art exhibit on the politics of memory entitled "Two 9/11s in a Lifetime," they taught me the possibilities of a collective creative endeavor. La Peña Cultural Center in Berkeley, California, is a home away from my home in Los Angeles. I learned so much from spending time with exiles there, at parties, in their homes, in informal conversations. Though the center never became a sustained focus of my inquiry, the experiences and conversations I enjoyed there and with its constituencies have been truly foundational for this project. Susana Kaiser has been a wonderful mentor and friend throughout.

I have been most fortunate to be welcomed to the University of Southern California by an astounding community of scholars. I am truly grateful for the guidance and close friendship of Ruth Wilson Gilmore, Laura Pulido, David Román, Judith Jackson Fossett, Pierrette Hondagneu-Sotelo, Dorinne Kondo, Sharon Hayes, George Sanchez, Mike Messner, Tim Biblarz, Fred Moten, and Leland Saito. Laura Harris and Alejandra Marchesky have been exceptional allies through difficult times. David Lloyd has deepened my understanding of intellectual community. Kelly Musick, Amon Emeka, Josh Kun, Clara Irazábal, Karen Tongson, Jane Iwamura, Janelle Wong, Ricardo Ramírez, and Sarah Banet-Weiser are wonderful colleagues and friends. I thank them for their patience, encouragement, and above all their friendship. In addition, I am privileged to work with a group of extremely talented graduate students in the American Studies and Ethnicity and the Sociology departments, and I am especially thankful to Micaela Smith, Gretel Vera, Araceli Esparza, Viet Le, Evren Savci, Suzel Bozada-Deas, and Cenk Ozbay. I owe a heartfelt thanks to Suzel, Evren, and Cenk for engaging with ideas and caring so deeply about scholarship and its potential impact. I thank Mica for careful research assistance.

I benefited enormously from presenting early versions of the work in many venues. Especially valuable was the feedback from Dorinne Kondo and the students of her American Studies and Ethnicity graduate seminar in cultural readings at the University of Southern California. A special thanks to Kathleen McHugh of the Center for the Study of Women at the University of California, Los Angeles, and to Sarah Banet-Weiser, Judith Halberstam, and Raquel Gutiérrez of the Center for Feminist Research at USC. I'm also grateful to John Carlos Rowe for inviting me to participate in the Transnational Americas conference held at USC in 2006. At UC Press, Naomi Schneider, Rose Vekony, and Susan Silver were extraordinary to work with during the editorial process. I also thank Michael Slosek of the press for detailed and very helpful assistance.

As I've come to know in embodied ways now, sustaining a book-length project to its completion requires many kinds of friends. Many thanks to new friends Yvonne Kelly and Dominic Moore for their passion and belief in me, and also for their reminders to live in the body, though, as I tell them, the mind is also a good place to dwell. Lorena Gómez-Barris and Eric Rocher have shared their home and heart with me, always. Lorena has been sister extraordinaire and assisted me with research, visually documenting many of the sites I describe. Vicente Gómez-Barris and Virginia Ramírez always took good care of me in small and large ways when I was in Chile, another second home.

I dedicate this work to those who were disappeared and to those who suffered greatly from the brutality of the Pinochet years. There are so many whose presence I've felt with me, whose nightmares have awoken me, whose struggles I have learned about through the bodies of the living, and whose resistance during a decisive historical period has mattered, setting an extraordinary example for my generation. Though my relationship with Salvador Allende Gossens has always been a mediated one, in many ways I consider him my spiritual father. His memory has been a blessed legacy in my life, and in the lives of so many others. I also dedicate this book to Renato Emile and Amalia Ixchel; I'm filled with wonder to call them my children. As I watch them embrace life, they continually remind me of the importance of renewing one's committed practice to social justice, and the imperative of working toward a profound understanding of past and present wrongs. As we know, both are necessary so that the promise of imagined futures may be, or continue to be, realized.

Ice and Political Heat

Cultural Memory Mediates the Past

The year 1992 marked many momentous local and global events, including the Seville World Fair. As a site of meaning five hundred years later, Seville, through the theme "Age of Discoveries," attempted to put a positive and colorful spin on the origin of what Aníbal Quijano (1997a, 1997b), Walter Mignolo (2000, 2005), and others have productively defined as the coloniality of power, the colonial origin story of deadly rupture in the Western Hemisphere beginning in 1492.[1] Through rehearsing the tropes of colonialism, most instrumentally by re-creating the voyages of the *Niña*, the *Pinta*, and the *Santa Maria*, Spanish leaders fashioned the dense event, process, and death project of colonization into a national and global media event. In the articulation of race(ism) and power, culture was mobilized as a strategy and resource made to compete against national integrationist paradigms. Culture was a key arena for the selective management of colonial history toward producing a stable national culture in unstable times. In the aftermath of the regional isolation left by the Franco dictatorship, and in a transitional moment toward defining itself through national, European, and global integration, Spain viewed the Seville World Fair as an important site of historical retelling with presentist ends in mind.

By hosting the World Fair in Seville, alongside the 1992 Summer Olympics in Barcelona, Spanish elites worked to rebrand Spain's national image through totems of glorious pasts.[2] Spain's image had been plagued by violence, Franco's thirty-six year regime, the subsequent fragile democracy, and uneven integration into the European economy. Drawing on the symbols of Seville's golden era as a nexus of colonial cultural and economic exchange, the Spanish government seized the moment to showcase the region's promising future, both as a hub of technology and as an emergent metropolis. The spectacle of "Discovery" at the Seville World Fair was mobilized as a cultural resource used to tame subaltern recognition and dissent (the counterhegemonic scripting of "Conquest" and colonization by indigenous activists as five hundred years of resistance), while favorably resituating Spain within the geopolitical map of global capitalism. It was, as Yúdice might have it, an expedient use of culture in the accelerated era of globalization (2005).

In the 1992 material and representational struggles over future possibilities, an iceberg from Chile had an equally symbolic and supporting role to play on the world stage, even while it was perhaps less spectacular. In an effort to rehabilitate the country's international image, tarnished by its legacy of authoritarianism, Chilean elites sent an iceberg from Patagonian waters to the Seville World Fair. Indeed, moving an iceberg over such a large distance required immense faith in refrigeration and streamlined bureaucratic export systems, twin icons of Pinochet's economic model, based on exporting fresh fruit for the world market (Petras and Leiva 1994). In one sense, the iceberg advertised Chile's capacity to transport perishables to Europe during the off-season, signaling to global elites that the country's neoliberal economic model would continue without so much as a ripple.[3] Spain's ex-colony Chile was also eager to distance itself from its image of authoritarian excess in order to *empujar* the transition toward political democracy after General Augusto Pinochet's regime, which lasted from 1973 to 1990.[4] In so doing, it alternately addressed, managed, reconciled, and obfuscated the violent excesses of the military junta.

Indeed, in the early 1990s, Chilean political democracy was a fragile enterprise, as many scholars have noted (Drake and Jaksic 1995; Winn 2004; Portales 2000). Pinochet still held his post as commander in chief of the military forces and had appointed himself *senador vitalicio* (senator for life). The principal obstacle of the time for "democratizing elites" was the distorted constitution, which in 1980 had been revised by Pinochet and the generals Merino, Mendoza, and Leigh to include a ban on union activity and, unsurprisingly, a grant of amnesty to state perpetrators through the 1978 Amnesty Law. As Villalobos-Ruminott states, "the amnesty procedure[s] soon revealed their efficacy, redirecting official discourse towards an ill-fated politics of impunity that appealed to well-publicized Chilean economic success to legitimize the dictum that proposed 'forgetting the errors of the past,' reconciling ourselves to the present, and advancing together united in a process of modernization and national development" (2000, 232). The legal framework for these alterations bounded up and hollowed the transition to political democracy, perpetuating the external image of Chile as a nation where the prosecution of atrocities could be at least temporarily suspended, while also laying the groundwork for the erasure of systematic atrocities from the nation's institutional memory, at least for the time being.

For critics of the transition to democracy and how it was handled, the iceberg (named *el blanqueo* or, literally, "whitening") was equated with historical erasure and analyzed as an archetype of "the economic miracle" (Moulian 1997; Richard 1998; Villalobos-Ruminott 2000). As sociologist and former Chilean presidential candidate Tomás Moulian expresses, the compulsion to forget and block the dictatorship past was in fact what defined the new democracy, at least in its early years (1997, 31).[5] Like the National Commission for Truth and Reconciliation's Rettig Report (1991) that circulated the first year after the transition, the iceberg became an icon in the quest by elites to distance the nation from the bloody past and to stake out a niche for its democracy in the era of globalization.[6] The iceberg display at the Seville World Fair metonymically signified the nation's desire to submerge the dirty work of the regime in an effort to showcase emergence in the global capitalist market. Interestingly, the colonial power and the ex-colony did not differ too widely in their belief in a global meritocracy, where new technology offered the possibility for national prowess, competition, and capitalist accumulation, rebranding nations through the erasure of violence. In this sense, both nations embodied Giorgio Agamben's notion of the spectacular state, whereby new states become legitimized through spectacles of erasure (2000, 75, 84–85).[7]

I open with this story about the iceberg and rebranding of both Chile and Spain to illuminate how the mobilization of national symbols can reveal historical processes of memory-making and forgetting. In the case of Chile, what was unseen or blocked by the glacier's apparent transparency? What remained hidden within the nation's mass graves, human rights archives, and national subconscious, covered up by the iceberg's long shadow and slow melting? Literary critic Lauren Berlant offers the term *national symbolic* to describe how nations mediate the national public through an "entangled cluster" of texts, which serve as links through which national identity is constructed and consolidated (1991, 1997). This is a relationship I expand on more fully in the subsequent sections, but for now want to suggest that the process of national identification gains traction through a kind of selectivity that condenses particular meaning formations, while banishing others from public visibility. Building on Berlant's work, I use the term *memory symbolic* to indicate how the national public sphere in transition is mediated and constructed by state-led initiatives (truth commissions, reports, commemorative events, memorials) and alternative forms of memory that reconstruct the past (gatherings of witnesses, public funerals, memorials) with presentist interests in mind. These are forms of memory that capture, disentangle, subdue, refuse, dilute, and otherwise tell the story of the authoritarian past and its legacies.[8] On the part of the state these are often symbolic strategies that assist in the process of smoothing over painful memories on the path toward national unity, strategies that in the case of Chile have aided the process of legitimizing capitalist restructuring.

Memory symbolics can be mobilized to selectively manage history in ways that reproduce state hegemony, reinscribing national identity in the fragility *after* collective violence. Alternative memory symbolics, however, can challenge and cast doubt on these limited renditions by suggesting that memory-making is complex, fluid, unending, and incomplete; it can construct, rather than merely flatten, human agency.[9] The iceberg is not the only such memory symbolic that has worked to obstruct the force of memory in the nation; this book is replete with examples. It is also replete with memory symbolics that untangle the stories of those who encountered state repression and its lingering afterlife in the nation and beyond. Although I also invoke the term *aftermath*, mostly to describe political and economic legacies, I find the term *afterlife* to be closer to the material struggles and realities endured by populations living through political violence. Therefore, I define the *afterlife* of political violence as the continuing and persistent symbolic and material effects of the original event of violence on people's daily lives, their social and psychic identities, and their ongoing wrestling with the past in the present.[10]

CULTURAL MNEMONICS

Starting from the rupture and afterlife of large-scale physical, psychic, and symbolic violence (Robben and Suárez-Orozco 2000),[11] I examine the afterlife of the Chilean dictatorship in the cultural arena. One of my central objectives is to note how the cultural realm is often a critical arena of struggle, engagement, and identification, where the past gives vitality and social meaning for the present to those directly affected by violence. This point follows what Raymond Williams discusses as a critical approach that "instead of reducing works to finished products and activities to fixed positions, is capable of discerning in good faith, the finite but significant openness of many actual initiatives and contributions" (1977, 114). In advocating Williams's fluid concept of hegemony as "a realized complex of experiences, relationships, and activities, with specific and changing pressures and limits," Michael Renov identifies how cultural analysis must "seek to comprehend the dynamic, ever-shifting conditions of significations without enthroning the process itself as a mystifying continuity" (2004, 5). Herein lies the challenge of examining cultural memory, where artists, their works, and audience engagement reshape and animate contemporary society. Working in the vein of cultural sociology, Lyn Spillman offers a valuable and accessible way to think about culture and its analysis, which prompts a parallel to the study of memory.[12] In this view, culture is defined as a process of meaning-making, where the "variable enactment of symbolic repertoires" creates and "allows for difference and conflict within and between social groups" (2005, 9). In parallel fashion, culture and memory are both terrains where meaning is constantly under negotiation, and it is through culture that shared meaning of memory is given salience.[13] Iwona Irwin-Zarecka contends that meaning of the past "is motivated by our experience but facilitated (or impeded) by public offerings. A 'collective memory'— as a set of ideas images, feelings about the past—is best located not in the minds of individuals, but in the resources they share" (1994, 4). It is through the gathering of individual memory threads and reconstituted social experience that symbolic memory repertoires accrue and inscribe meaning to negotiate the past in contemporary society.

Representations of political violence, such as memorials, peace parks, documentary film, and visual art, contain important clues about the afterlife and memory of violence. These are the "media of memory" where the persistence of the past makes itself felt in the present (Stier 2003). Cultural production does not provide mere repositories, reflections, and expressions of the force

of the past in the present, for they are also productive sites of social meaning where societies deal with, contest, struggle over, represent, and continue their journey through rupture. Elizabeth Jelin
proposes that memories are "subjective processes anchored in experiences and in symbolic and material markers" (2003, xv), where
representational sites can unveil the different meanings attached
to the past in the locus of the present. In fact, as Stier explains,
"memory, history and society are . . . entangled, and nowhere is
this more evident than in the cultural realm" (2003, 8). Culture,
then, not only offers a view into the past but is constitutive of
that very past in ways that thread together and pull apart social
worlds.

The notion of collective memory as a shared enterprise that is
performed in cultural production set the stage for my initial research questions: What do symbolics of memory tell us about its
afterlife? How do these representations offer and negotiate meaning about the experiences of collective violence in the nation? To
answer these questions, I traveled to Chile on five separate occa-
sions for field research from 1998–2004, living there for a period
of a year in total. I conducted research in human rights archives
primarily in Santiago, including at the Fundación de Documentación y Archivo de la Vicaría de la Solidaridad (Foundation for
Documentation and Archives of the Vicarage of Solidarity), an
impressive collection where more than eighty thousand legal documents, victims' testimonials, eyewitness accounts, and visual materials are housed, and at the smaller yet substantive archives of
the Fundación Salvador Allende and the Agrupación de Familiares de Detenidos Desaparecidos (Association of Relatives of the
Detained and Disappeared).[14] I also conducted ethnographic and
participant research at numerous countermemory sites through-

Figure 1. Installation memorial to the disappeared and a mural honoring Father Juan Alsina (detail). A view from Puente Bulnes on the Mapocho River, June 18, 2002. Photo by Nicole Hayward.

out the urban center. The striking memorials at Puente Bulnes are but one of dozens of sites that did not become central to my archival work, interviews, ethnography, and textual analysis (fig. 1). Here, a wall memorial, a mural, a collage project, and more traditional religious and memorial elements, such as plaques, crosses, and flowers, converge to produce a layered and multileveled viewpoint of terror's memory. Though I did not choose this site as a subject of sustained inquiry, the unsettling collage, where faded portraits of those who were disappeared hang over the Mapocho River, has stayed with me throughout this project as an aesthetic imprint that, despite weathering, refuses erasure.[15]

Through my site work I found that one partial answer to my

research questions on state terror, its afterlife, and representational meaning is that large-scale violence, and in particular authoritarianism, creates new forms of exclusion and thus new forms of social participation and identification. Therefore two subsequent research questions emerged in my analysis of cultural production: What subjectivities, or how people identify in the social world, and intersubjectivities, or the way people identify in the social world with each other, does state violence help to produce? How do sites of representation of collective violence help constitute and otherwise make apparent these social identities?

My position as researcher was often as an outsider, although as a second-generation Chilean I had insider knowledge about how memory constructs identities, personal meaning that when narrated and creatively embodied produces sociality. In California, in both the Bay Area (San Francisco and Oakland) and in Southern California (Los Angeles and San Diego), I participated as an "insider" in exile cultural events throughout a three-year period from 2001–2004, which provided insights that find their way into the contents of this book's conclusion. Throughout the research, site work, and writing process, both at the sites and afar, textual, visual and interpretative analysis have been critical components and integral to my sociological imagination that incorporates multiple methodologies in the difficult effort to approximate imposed disaster and its attendant consequences.[16]

Since 1997, the year sociologist Tomás Moulian's *Chile actual: Anatomía de un mito* (Chile Today: Anatomy of a Myth) was published, dozens of books and articles in cultural magazines have discussed both the distinctive character of democracy as amnesiac about the violent past, and the subaltern spaces in which memory lingers (Richard 1998, 2000, 2001; Lira 2000, 2001; Illanes 2002).[17] My own contribution extends this important scholarship by telling a story about sites of ruptured memory and the process of rescue, transmutation, and recovery. I view cultural memory as archival fragments, as memory symbolics, as sites of disaster, and as ways to understand the persistence of state terror in people's lives, bodies, and subjectivities. Although these cultural productions have different degrees of mobility and circulation, they share an imagination about state terror that begins from the perspective of those most affected in the nation. These productions include Villa Grimaldi, a clandestine concentration camp turned into a memorial site; *Fernando ha vuelto* (Fernando Returns), a 1998 documentary film by Silvio Caiozzi about the remains of a man who was a husband, brother, and Allende sympathizer; and the body of work by painter and torture survivor Guillermo Núñez. From outside Chile, I also consider the transnational exilic dimension of cultural memory as seen in an art exhibit and event on the politics of memory in the San Francisco Bay Area, home of La Peña Cultural Center.[18]

Though my focus is on representation, state terror effects must necessarily be situated within the frame of collective mnemonics. Joining other studies that theorize and argue for contending with the haunting legacies of torture, disappearance, and the massive violence through cultural sites and their meaning (Gordon 1997; Robben 1995, 1996, 2000; Straker et al. 1992; Wagner-Pacifici and Schwartz 2002; Young 1993; Sturken 1997; Nelson 2002; Coombes 2003; Stier 2003), I focus on visual representations and physical spaces that relate to important political historical genres (political art), offer an engagement with audiences (documentary film), and map the collective subjectivities of state terror and its afterlife (memorial parks). Methodologically, I show how the sociality of cultural places and productions are important deposits of memory, logical places to turn to for evidence of the relationships between collective violence and national refashioning, as well as its effects.

The social projections, use, meanings, and mobilizations of cultural sites uncover effects on group identities over time. Along these lines, Jeffrey Olick discusses how collective memory "refers to the group's sense of itself as a continuous entity through times, as well as to the manifestations of, and efforts to enhance, that sense of continuity" (2007, 86). This sense of continuity touches down through mediation. Marita Sturken notes that cultural memory "is a field of contested meanings in which Americans interact with cultural elements to produce concepts of the nation, particularly in events of trauma, where both the structures and the fractures of a culture are exposed" (1997, 2–3). In a similar vein, I show how cultural production not only is a repository of social reality but also plays an active role in constituting meaning toward a field of identification and memory. The work of memory and identity at the collective level leads us to the analytical scale of nations and nation-states that have a particular purchase on referencing group identity.

MEMORY-NATIONS, EXCLUSION, AND STATE VIOLENCE

Given that symbolic enactments produce systems of meaning in a nation, in periods of transition various performances of memory, such as memorialization, truth-telling processes, and so forth, create the symbolic repertoire for the reconstruction of national identity. Max Weber defines the features of the nation-state simply as a political community based on a common language or culture in close relation to power, linking the nation to the state (1978, 1:325). Weber also identifies the nation as a community of memories, suggesting that the past forges crucial social bonds within a national territory through feelings of adhesion to the abstract entity that is the nation (1978, 1:398). These bonds are reinforced through constructions and narratives of the past, and through the selection of particular histories. As Benedict Anderson comments, the nation promotes membership through common bonds of an "imagined community," a delimited territory that is sovereign (1991, 6).[19]

Like memory itself, the nation-state functions through the process of selection and also through a series of exclusions. One of the most pivotal exclusions turns on the construction of the citizen-subject. As philosopher Giorgio Agamben underscores, the nation-state's sovereignty is instantiated through the citizen-subject, which at birth replaces the attribute of human as the primary condition of being (2000, 20–21). Therefore, citizen becomes a quintessential locator for national subjects and legal processes that emerge with the "birth of the nation," which forcefully produce hierarchies between social groups.[20] Many have also characterized these exclusions as the nation-state's inherent denial of sexual and racial difference (Balibar 1994, 58; Anthias and Yuval-Davis 1992; Omi and Winant 1994; Alarcón, Kaplan, and Moallem 1999). Through marginalized subjects, the nation-state constitutes and polices its boundaries to define itself, a hegemonic process that exacts new forms of consent to continually maintain the fiction of a containable and "governable" entity. Indeed, the nation is made possible and expressed through cultural and political means wherein borders (between subjects, geographical entities, and histories) construct it as a homogenous, stable, and enduring geopolitical entity. Though national subjects are conditioned to view the nation as fixed, nations are in fact phantasmatic and inherently unstable productions. Nations also structure subjects' ability to belong.[21] In this light, the nation is a project that is always made, challenged, and remade through exclusionary practices as much as through inclusionary structures of meaning. Just as nations create the desire to belong, they use violence to target who is cast as marginal in the national project of reconstruction.

These entry points into nation allow me to analyze the macrostructural project of authoritarianism and its transition to political democracy. Rather than the outcome of decisions made by a few rogue military men, Chile's authoritarian regime was the byproduct of centuries of social exclusion by elite classes and the culmination of profound social challenges to that exclusion. A medical doctor who had served as Minister of Health (1939–1941) and held various elected offices, socialist politician Salvador Allende unsuccessfully ran for president in 1952, 1958, and 1964. By 1964, social unrest had made its presence on the national scene. In particular, the grave structural and economic divides between rural landless peasants and the owners of latifundios, estates in a colonial system that had persisted for more than four hundred years, took center stage in the presidential race of that year. The hemispheric system of influence ensured that the United States would pour millions of dollars into the middle-of-the-road, reform-oriented Christian Democratic candidate Eduardo Frei, who ran on the platform of land reform, in contrast to Allende's more radical promise to dismantle the serious inequities of the latifundio system in Chile through land redistribution. Six years later, Chile's working classes would no longer be content with a modest plan of reform, and despite a close race, a massive social movement propelled Allende to the presidency in 1970.[22]

Allende's substantive program was to redistribute wealth and land in Chile, mainly through increasing wages by about forty percent while keeping the prices of goods static and, significantly, by nationalizing the copper industry and the bank system. These policies outraged the elite classes and multinational interests, who retaliated through a series of national and international boycotts and political complications that ultimately paralyzed the nation. Allende's political action had made visible the social fractures that existed in the nation and the degree to which the elite classes in Chile had sustained their privilege on the backs of the poorest and most marginal sectors.[23] By 1973, with inflation at an all-time high, the revolution had been preempted by powerful economic and ideological interests, and rumors of a military "solution" to political and economic turmoil ran high. On September 11, 1973, President Allende's socialist path was truncated by a military coup, which led to Allende's death. Human rights violations became the primary mode of dismantling all that Allende's dream of social equality entailed. Efforts by popular classes to gain access to the privileges of citizenship through the short-lived Allende presidency (1970–1973) were effectively shut down by those conditioned to police and maintain social, class, and color hierarchies.

Even long after the dictatorship's end in 1990, political democracy in Chile continued to exclude from the nation the social subjects it had fractured during the period of state violence. This was a twofold process: First, authoritarianism expelled those at the other end of the state's accusatory finger and war machine from the "political community" through imprisonment and banishment. The specific subjects of my study are those who have been tortured, those disappeared and their relatives, and those forced into exile. Second, during political transitions, exclusions formed the basis for the system of political democracy, in many ways stripping aggrieved groups of their rights as citizens, while also transforming them into symbolic occupiers of grievance that functioned to consolidate the transition. This is no more true than in the figure of the grieving mother, the widow, and the *compañera* whose loss in Southern Cone dictatorships has stood in for the transitional nation.[24] Female subjectivity in this instance is literally fused with victimization despite these women's activism and protest, which I detail in chapter 4. Part of the complexity of this omission is that it is based on prior exclusions, again forming a double boundary; that is, those detained, tortured, and disappeared were first the most disenfranchised subjects of the nation (working-class, indigenous, female, queer).

During the transition to political democracy, especially in the early period, these subjects still did not belong to the nation, since many spheres continued to be minimally democratized. Democracy, as the standard term that is used in the literature is "minimally, a governmental system that provides for peaceful competition for positions of power at regular intervals, open participation in the election of leaders and policies, and civil and political liberties that ensure the legitimacy of competition and participation" (Paley 2001, 3). As Julia Paley observes, there are many descriptions of what Chile's democracy has been. The most provocative that circulated in the public sphere include "*democracia restringida* (restricted democracy), *democracia cupular* (elite democracy), *democracia lite* (low-fat democracy), and *democracia entre comillas* (democracy in quotation marks)."

A more expanded treatment rethinks the limited terms of a political democracy that constrains contemporary and historical agency. To summarize these constraints, I would argue that those affected by state-sponsored terror had little legal or formal recourse, exemplified by a fraught and stacked court system and constitutional restraints, which dramatically limited any possibility for citizenship participation in a traditional sense. In its effort to rebrand the nation as a global capitalist player, the state again reproduced exclusion, whereby dead, damaged, and disappeared bodies became the debris of capitalist restructuring.[25] Thus, the state created new market subjects and citizens by erasing the memory and subjectivity of the dead, the tortured, and other survivors.

There is one final theoretical frame that cannot be vanished. Dead bodies come from the labyrinths of the interlocking systems of empire and state violence. As Menjívar and Rodríguez have argued (2005, 4) and as countless declassified CIA documents now make clear, political violence and authoritarianism in Latin America during the 1970s and 1980s can be attributed, at least in part, to U.S. dominance in the regional system.[26] These authors note how state violence cannot be exclusively explained as a legacy of colonialism, since the rational and bureaucratized character of terror is consistent with the Weberian model of a modern nation embedded within the exigencies of a global system. Indeed, state-sponsored terror works through the modern political system of bureaucratic societies (Rejali 1994; Menjívar and Rodríguez 2005). State violence enacts, through the framework of the modern nation-state, the empire's and national elite's effort to maintain and expand hegemony.

MODERNITY AND FORMS OF KNOWING

As scholars have commented, the contemporary character of memory in Chile is fragmentary, yet for all its lapses, memory remains ubiquitous (Huyssen 1995; Nora 1992; Olick 2003). It also leaves traces. Jeffrey Olick notes a historical shift with respect to memory: "Where premodern societies lived within the continuous past, contemporary societies have separated memory from the continuity of social reproduction; memory is now a matter of explicit signs, not of implicit meanings" (2003, 3). Olick suggests that postmodern memory is constructed from residues, a point that leads us back to the question of the afterlife of violence. Memory's trace is a materially embodied image of the violence of modernity. Indeed, World War II, with the Jewish Holocaust and the atomic bombings of Nagasaki and Hiroshima, is the quintessential period that makes evident how modernity erupts as violence. The remnants of the Holocaust, which include ashes, hair, and the remains of shoes from ovens and gas chambers in Nazi camps, materialize, however obliquely, to make their claim on the past. Such artifacts constitute what Stier calls "Holocaust icons," or those objects that stand witness to horrific events and communicate a piece of their enormity. These pieces of lives lost, such as a child's shoes, red and gray and black shoes, leggings, slippers, and so forth,[27] are all ghostly representations that signal modern atrocity.[28] However, their visual display cannot ensure that we are somehow getting closer to the matter of living through, or perishing from, something as unfathomable as the Holocaust experience. Scholarly analysis requires paying close attention to what these traces say about modern forms of power.

Sketching the effects of many forms of modernity's violence,

Avery Gordon describes the haunting by the inevitable and often untamable ghosts of modernity (Marx's ghost in the machine) that are a constitutive feature of social life (1997, 7). For Gordon, ghostly matters are those things that are unseen and therefore difficult to measure, but that are nevertheless a seething presence in the social world. In many ways, the concept of ghostly matters is an entrance point for discussing the complexity of social worlds and the difficulty of rendering them through conventional disciplinary approaches, which is why Gordon gestures to the importance of interdisciplinary work.[29] Ghostly matters produce hauntings, the traces of power on subjects and their social world. Therefore, how do we make knowledge that does not foreclose the rich texture of social life?

Gordon's notion of ghostly matters creates a multivalent conceptual frame that allows me to stage three of the book's themes. First, ghostly matters are those themes that are either absent from power's purview or conditioned and banished into invisibility. Second, ghostly matters challenge the compartmentalization of knowledge that is overly invested in the empirical. Gordon writes that "the real itself and its ethnographic or sociological representations are also fictions, albeit powerful ones that we do not experience as fictional, but as true" (11). These are the multiple modes of representation embedded within the constitution of the "real" that are needed to escape from, or at least to see, these epistemological pitfalls. Third, ghostly matters are about complex subjectivity. Tracking complex personhood requires an understanding of how the social world is discursively constructed, as well as "an engagement with the social structuring practices that have long been the province of sociological inquiry. It is these that draw our attention to the multiple determination and sites of power in which narratives of and about our culture and its artifacts are produced and disseminated" (11). Gordon continues, "If we want to study social life well, and if in addition we want to contribute, in however small a measure, to changing it, we must learn how to identify hauntings and reckon with ghosts, must learn how to make contact with what is without doubt often painful, difficult, and unsettling" (23). In studying the afterlife of atrocity, I take as central Gordon's points about what is vanished, the "real" of complex subjectivity. Representation offers an entry into these three themes. Memory symbolics also offers a way to think about conditions of historical knowledge and agency after violence, engaging aspects of the social sciences and the humanities as critical access points by which to address traces.

In her stunning work on the memoryscape of Hiroshima in the aftermath of the atom bomb, Lisa Yoneyama similarly addresses the possibility for historical agency and knowledge in a way that bridges the objective/subjective divide of modern disciplines on the one hand, and postmodernist and deconstructionist critique on the other. Memory becomes a form of mediation that does not immediately discount the possibility for individual agency within the historical structures that postmodernism has sometimes suggested (1999, 33). As Yoneyama asserts, "By formulating the question of historical knowledge in terms of memory, and by illuminating its constructed and mediated nature, we can determine more precisely the conditions of power that shape the ways in which that past is conveyed and ask how such representations interpolate and produce subjects" (ibid.). Historical agency can be imagined through how the past is reinterpreted and renarrated in contemporary conditions. This leads to a central epistemological inquiry of my book: if management and concealment are primary modes of hegemonic historical transitions, where indeed can memory be found?[30]

In her work on postapartheid South Africa, Coombes explores how visual culture is the starting place for an analysis of memory and nation building, where social fractures loom large in the attempt to redefine the nation. Coombes analyzes nationally visible cases that highlight the debates over culture within the public sphere during the early remaking of the nation; these "possibilities on offer" by artists show the range of imaginaries in the new period (2003). As scholar Mieke Bal puts it, cultural analysis differs from history in that it "is based on a keen awareness of the critic's situatedness in the present, the social and cultural present from which we look, and look back, at the objects that are always already of the past, objects that we take to define our present culture" (1999, 1). In reading film, memorials, and paintings as social texts, I follow a tradition in sociology and cultural studies, indebted to Durkheim, where the social world is viewed as a system of signs whose meaning can be interpreted (Seidman 1997, 43). My analysis of cultural objects as social expression follows this view to acknowledge how society is "deeply cultural or . . . organized by signs and meanings patterned in relations of identity and difference" (ibid.). In other words, I discuss practices of and conflict produced by visual mediums within the particular cultural and social milieu of Chile. As Michael Emmison and Philip Smith outline, researching the visual has often been "marginalized from the core concerns of social sciences" (2000, 2). Much is lost without visual analysis to track the effects of authoritarianism in people's lived daily encounter with structures and to illustrate how these constitute meaningful social relations toward deeper democratic possibilities. In fact, through gestures, icons, metonyms, abstraction, and so forth, the visual is some-times the only archive of what is better left unfound and unsaid.[31] In this sense, the visual register often adds important dimensions to written testimonials, creating archives that function as excep-tions to the culture of silence so present in the afterlife of col-lective violence.

Even while the intersections of the work on trauma and cul-tural memory are useful and generative for the postauthoritarian period in Chile, it is beyond the scope of my book to rehearse the vast and continually expanding literatures and conceptual fram-ings on the topic.[32] How can memory be analytically approximated in a manner that does not, as Todorov would ask, abuse its origin? Critic María Teresa Rojas tells us that art, as with other cultural sites, can be the voice of official memory or an alternative to it (M. T. Rojas 2000, 299). I believe this classic binary in memory literature between official memory and countermemory as two opposing sites of contention, representation, and possibility oc-cludes important gradations in terms of the labor that cultural pro-duction and symbols perform.[33] In part, this is a question about the limits of epistemologies as modes of understanding the past that cannot apprehend, beyond binary analytics, how memory can be constitutively constructed. In this book I make explicit how these cultural productions constitute, fashion, rehearse, and oth-erwise contend with the memory of collective violence.

SKETCHES OF THE PAST

Although Allende's socialist project had been under sustained at-tack by global and national conservatives since its inception, Sep-tember 11, 1973, marked the beginning of the end of a political dream that involved millions of people who had worked to create revolutionary and cultural change through *poder popular*.[34] The military takeover that dramatically overturned the socialist path in Chile was initially accomplished by bombing La Moneda Presidential Palace and through the death of democratically elected President Salvador Allende.[35] With a cast of characters that included Richard Nixon, Henry Kissinger, the CIA, Chilean elites and their puppets, U.S. imperialist and cold war ideologies and policies pushed national conditions until they "screamed."[36] This momentous time was a national, and perhaps global, historical shift and irrevocable breach, certainly not singular in its importance but at least pivotal at that particular juncture of world political change and collective social possibility. Allende was a charismatic leader who offered, like Simón Bolívar, José Martí, and others, a hopeful if fully unrealized civil rights and economic agenda for the nation and a politically democratic revolutionary path for the Americas. In stark contrast, the military resolution that generals Merino, Mendoza, Leigh, and Pinochet imposed came to embody a social, economic, and cultural nightmare, perhaps more in line with the autocratic tendencies of the nation that continue to haunt Chilean social and political realities.[37] The truncated dreams of U.S. black civil rights leaders and the assassinations of Malcolm X and Dr. Martin Luther King can be referenced to describe the terrible breach that Salvador Allende's death and subsequent state terror produced, not only for national supporters, but also for individuals and social movements around the planet. For instance, it is still common to hear detailed accounts, almost like flashbulb memories, of where people were when they heard the end of Allende's final broadcast transmitted by Radio Magallanes: "Long live Chile! Long live the people! Long live the workers! These are my last words. I am sure that my sacrifice will not be in vain; I am sure that it will at least be a moral lesson which will punish felony, cowardice and treason" (Cockcroft 2000, 242). Abductions, collective graves, disappearances, military curfews, torture, media censorship, forced exile, and a generalized climate of fear followed the military coup. Poor urban communities, such as Pintera outside Santiago, were effectively occupied by military forces, leading to bitter and deadly street battles that have marked the political perspectives, structural opportunities, and social identities of subsequent generations.

In a process that took many years, but was especially acute in the seventies and early eighties, violence was used against Allende activists and sympathizers as a means to disarticulate mass social mobilizations and to install a counterrevolutionary project. Especially in the first period, from 1973–1978, many exiles who fled the country, including my family members and family friends, had been victims of concentration camps that were set up around Chile, were forced into hiding, and were under constant persecution and surveillance by the military. Their homes were subject to random ransacking and their families were threatened. In short, millions witnessed and bore the extremes of collective effervescence and complete rupture in a very short window of time, with grave consequences for social and individual being.

One of the key ideologies and practices of authoritarianism was the dramatic turn toward privatization and deregulation, where the state rescinded its social contract with its citizens. Beginning in 1974, Chile was in many respects the global test case for neoliberalism as Pinochet's dictatorship was characterized as "one of the most comprehensive free market restructurings ever attempted worldwide" (Paley 2001, 7).[38] This was to form the main engine of continuity in the transition period. As authoritarianism increasingly came under local, regional, national, and international pressure in the 1980s and 1990s for its overt human rights violations, nations began to shift toward "democratic governments." In so doing they were faced with stepped-up pressure to instill or continue free market principles from the "Washington Consensus," the compendium of global lending institutions dominated by the United States. In his inaugural speech, Patricio Aylwin, the first president of Chile (1990–1994) after the return to political democracy, said that his main priority would be to deal with the human rights violations and address the "social debt" that neoliberal policies had accrued under Pinochet (1997, 152). Aylwin chose to direct attention to the military and its "masculine spirit" as a representation of the nation, rather than propose an open and public process for addressing its abominable role in dictatorship violence, a position that was to continue with the publication of the National Commission for Truth and Reconciliation's Rettig Report in 1991. As he stated in the same speech, "Chile has always loved and admired its armed forces. It is identified with the nation's glory, with the masculine spirit of Chileans, and with the sacrificial actions it takes in daily life or in the context of grave emergencies. Bearing the cross of reconciliation in a truly united Chile requires the removal of obstacles that still prejudice those feelings" (ibid.). Reconciliation as a form of concealment operated through patriarchal pacts of transition, forcing closure over what had yet to be revealed.

ATTENDING TO CONCEALMENT

My book is a cautionary tale to other nations transitioning from authoritarian forms of political organization to democracy. Many states around the world, including Guatemala, Uruguay, Argentina, El Salvador, Vietnam, Peru, and South Africa have paid a high social price for sustaining structural inequality through terror, war, and apartheid. In reconstruction periods or in periods of transitions to democracy, nations that have experienced violence are forced to come to terms with the past and to engage a diverse group of citizens and victims into a new imaginary for the nation. Through truth commissions, reparations, and the processing of war criminals and peace accords, some contemporary postauthoritarian experiences of nation building have been successful at integrating the past into a new narrative and articulation of the national democratic project, but those individuals who have suffered the strong hand of power may never be able to stitch their lives together in a similar fashion. Reconciliation processes, "putting the past behind us," are central ways that governments get on with the business of reconstructing the nation, often at the expense of victims and their families. As subsequent chapters show, superficial approaches to reconciliation alone produce a project of nation making that is unsustainable, jeopardizing the core principles and practices of democracy. In other words, while power from above moves to close the issue of violence for the nation, from below the heterogeneous effects of violence constantly threaten to rupture and disarticulate the transitional national project.

This is nowhere more the case than in the subjectivities of those who have had to persist in the face of unspeakable violence. In one of those strange moments of fieldwork, I met Carmen Vivanco, an elderly survivor whose struggle and post-state violence identity itself are symbolic of the uneven and confounding memory processes in the nation. I was interviewing Viviana Díaz—a torture survivor, the daughter of a disappeared militant, and the current president of the internationally recognized Agrupación de Familiares de Detenidos Desaparecidos (AFDD)—when Vivanco, now in her eighties, slowly entered the room and brought us tea on a tray. I gasped as I recognized her image from Patricio Guzmán's now classic film *Chile, Obstinate Memory* (1997). In my mind, I quickly ran through the list of her disappeared family members, those she lists before the camera and who I know by memory after seeing the film dozens of times. Díaz turned to me as if to reassure me. After Vivanco left the room, Díaz told me that she came to the AFDD office every day, and had been doing so ever since the group's founding almost thirty years ago. After attending many events and visiting the office of the AFDD several times, I began to understand how relatives of the disappeared were family to each other, linked through a history of collective tragedy and personal loss. The close bonds formed by suffering have created an important human rights movement in Chile that continues to demand accountability. Carmen Vivanco's daily life, like that of the other mothers, wives, husbands, brothers, and sisters that form the core membership of the AFDD, is the expression of an identity produced out of the experience of dictatorship violence and incomplete justice in the democratic era.

In the early years of the transition in Chile, the Rettig Report, the release of white doves in the national stadium during President Aylwin's inauguration speech, the human rights discursive regime of "never again," and so on were all dramatic performances and rhetorical strategies by elite politicians to represent and therefore inaugurate a return to democracy as the new organization of the nation. For Southern Cone authoritarianism, the reconfiguration of national belonging has operated within cultures of impunity (Kaiser 2005), the diminished power of constitutionalism (Lira 2000), and radical economic restructuring, which includes the imposition and alleged triumph of capital over labor and labor's agency. All of these tactics work to enhance the social trauma of the dictatorship years and to block the memory of popular struggle and achievement during the Allende revolutionary project.

WHERE MEMORY DWELLS

One piece of the story I explore in the book is where memory is absent and whom it continues to disturb. The other piece is where it can be found, recuperated and even incorporated, though never fully, to expand state power. In conditions where extreme forms of physical, spiritual, psychological, and emotional destruction target collectivities (as do conquest, slavery, genocide, invasion, state violence, femicide, decimation of welfare, imprisonment/torture during late capitalism, the "War on Terror," AIDS and its politics, and so on), it is impossible to tame memory, since these events produce an excess that can never fully be incorporated into hegemonic projects. I have come to think about the "dwelling" of the memory of torture, disappearance, and forced exile—the central topics of this book—as a double entendre: as a literal "living with" and inhabitance of bodies, psyches, and spaces; and as a lingering presence, one that persists, insists, resists, and exceeds the containment of these bodies and of the nation's boundaries, the afterlife of the event of violence. Those memories that dwell go unperceived by a state in transition, since its very existence is oriented toward the future, eliding or making increasingly invisible the past in its effort to get beyond it. Illuminating where and how memories dwell in specific cultural locations allows for a "real-world" application of Benjamin's dialectics of memory, which centers historical knowledge as a force for present efforts toward social change.[39] How can we access memory's ephemeral and complex nature in situations of collective violence where experiences of loss, trauma, fracture, and instability are present? I contend that these experiences often accrue social visibility and audibility only through cultural production and representation. And it is precisely the accumulation and sociality of these memories that dwell, those memories emergent in cultural production, that may ultimately expose transitional states' efforts to force closure over violence and its afterlife.

Where Memory Dwells reflects a search for the memory of atrocities, both on a personal level and through my scholarly work. In my search for what happened to family members, family friends, and those that I have now come to include in my imaginary as part of my extended family, whether they be archival figures or people whose work and journeys I have come to know and deeply respect, cultural representation showed me the vivid afterlife of violence. My research into state terror and its effects posed great ethical challenges, both because of its painful and ephemeral content and because of the inherent difficulty in adequately writing about such matters. One of the ways I resolved the dilemma (and burden) of representation is by realizing for myself (and suggesting to the reader) that this is always a partial story, and one motivated by my own ironic position. I came to the United States as a young child under conditions of exile and, after living in the United States for more than thirty years, I finally decided to apply for citizenship only after holding a green card became insecure after the events of September 11, 2001.[40] Since my childhood, identification with the U.S. empire's audacity has conditioned my social and political perception and intellectual sensibilities. My return to the ghosts of Chile's violence has been accomplished only through a treacherous, partial, and deeply saddening journey to the other side of what was lost and what remains to be found. Another way I have addressed the research of what remains is by engaging the work of survivors, artists, docents, and scholars as an acknowledgment of the unfinished project of deconstruction and reconstruction. This is what sociologist Denise da Silva Ferreira thoughtfully suggested to me once as the work of generations of scholars.

Much of what follows analyzes forms of cultural memory that complicate the uneven story the nation has told through its institutional processes. In this sense, I cover the period of transition leading up to January 2006, when Michelle Bachelet, a torture survivor and daughter of General Bachelet (who died from a heart attack caused by his imprisonment), was elected president of Chile, beginning to overtly and in more subtle ways encode her discourses with testimonial gestures of her own experiences. The death of General Augusto Pinochet on December 10, 2006, coincidentally on International Human Rights Day, has unleashed other public memory formations from which future work on cultural memory can build on what I set forth here.

There have been important markers of memory in the nation, periods where the rupture of national silence have shifted public commentary and understanding. These markers follow temporal sequences as much as they do the political framework of the Concertación transition, which aimed to solidify capitalist economic and social hegemony. For instance, the thirty-year anniversary of Allende's overthrow, in 2003, marked a momentous shift in memory politics in the nation, where the floodgates of what had been a taboo public topic were thrown open in all forms of commemoration, tribute, memorial display, and so forth. And after years of little national recognition, Guillermo Núñez, the painter of torture scenes, received the prestigious 2007 National Prize of Fine Arts. It is important to state, then, that what I discuss in this book is based on shifting national conditions and possibilities for debate, and shifting uses and abuses of memory. These cultural productions are rich sites from which to understand what has been left out of the nation in transition and how geopolitical histories continue to impact transnational identity.

A nation of seventeen million people, Chile may seem marginal within U.S. sociology, but it has been a focus of U.S.-based Latin American Studies since even Allende's presidency.[41] The economic and political exigencies of globalization, much as the Cold War in an earlier moment, give an international focus particular currency. Although Chile was a pivotal country of political battles during the Cold War turmoil, representing in Henry Kissinger's eyes "the irresponsibility of its own citizens" (Burbach and Cantor 2004), as a story of counterrevolution it often resides outside the purview of centers of power, even while there are structural, material, and historical links to U.S. foreign policy and economic globalization.[42] Thus, the narrative of post-Allende Chile and the political transition in a U.S. context invokes a different form of historical memory.[43] In particular, using Latin American scholar Walter Mignolo's concept of border gnoseology, as knowledge from a subaltern perspective, which is "conceived from the exterior borders of the modern/colonial world system" (Mignolo 2000, 11), I work to make visible a counterhistory, within the contemporary global order, that disturbs and unsettles hierarchies of state and global power, intervention, national hierarchies, and historical memory through its force in people's lived experiences that emerge in cultural memory. Yoneyama, writing on the indelible traces and spatial articulations of memory in Hiroshima, notes that memory is a useful way to point out the constructedness of national and global histories (1999). Chile as an economic miracle and "democratic" government has been secured through global and national political arenas that eclipse the complexity of memory formations, writing out of history those who suffered in their bodies and minds the political heat of the Cold War and its long shadow.

WHILE I AM INTERESTED IN place and memorialization, in the following chapters I also think about visual culture, especially through memorial sites, art, and documentation. Chapter 2 discusses Villa Grimaldi, a former concentration camp turned Peace Park that has been preserved by a group of concerned witnesses, survivors, and human rights activists. This place was one site where the counterrevolution was won on the path to economic liberalization.[44] Places of extermination and torture, and their transformation during the transition to democracy, present a rich view of authoritarian rule and democratic consolidation. Unlike other concentration camps, mass graves, and prisons that constitute national symbols of atrocity, this memorial site has rarely been studied by scholars (Aguilar 1999, 2000; Richard 2001, Meade 2004). Yet it is one of the few sites of torture in Latin America that has been preserved as a memorial (Meade 2004, 193).[45] Like memorial sites that now have greater public recognition in Chile, it exists only through the work of a group of concerned activists and former prisoners who wanted to remember this brutal history in the public sphere and promote cultural activities that educate about state terror. I study Villa Grimaldi by incorporating little-known government documents and testimonies of the site (e.g., C. Rojas ca. 1981), while also providing a social, political, and cultural analysis of its present-day role in the nation. However, Villa Grimaldi is more than a story about Chile's dictatorship and the recuperation of memory. Through an analysis of the Villa Grimaldi concentration camp and the Peace Park, we get a better picture of the multiple modes of resistance and remembrance that, I argue, are fundamental and not contrary to the larger project of democracy in Latin America.

Similarly, as I discuss in chapter 3, in its logic and focus on matters of torture, Guillermo Núñez's abstract art manages to shine a spotlight onto the flawed and incomplete national processes of political democracy. I consider what Núñez's art says about the experience of torture to avail the social costs of authoritarianism and to expose social forgetting about whose bodies paid (and continue to pay) for Chile's global economic model. I focus on Núñez's blindfolded captivity, testimonial practice, and aesthetic interventions to argue that the experience of torture is not only relived daily, as the literature on trauma would suggest, but produces an impossibility of reattachment to national projects. The tortured subjects' dismemberment is never fully re-membered, perhaps until the terms of broad social justice are imagined and put into motion. Rather than being stuck in trauma's never ending cycle and in a static past, Núñez's subjective identification with torture and his aesthetic practices imagine a different past, one oriented toward the possibilities of democracy in the future.

Chapter 4 considers material disappearance and its cinematic witness during political violence in terms of those that remain. The act of disappearing a body can occur within a period of minutes, hours, or even months. It can happen through assassination, either through a single shot or through multiple gun wounds, with the body deposited into a collective and unmarked grave. Or disappearance can take place through slow, methodical torture that ultimately produces death and the dumping of the body, perhaps into the sea. Though the act of disappearance may vary, its effects continue over lifetimes. What happens to a family, to its members, *after* disappearance? Documentary can defamiliarize what we know or think we know about disappearance by revealing its effects on subjects' lives. I discuss the conventions, constructions, and silences of gender, military discourses, the family, burial, survival, and exile, and how documentary problematizes these issues when the subject is disappearance.

Before, during, and after the dictatorship, documentary film served variegated social and political purposes: First, documentaries archived the counterrevolution by the political Right, which culminated in President Allende's death, the death of a social dream, and the installation of the military dictatorship. Documentaries of these events have traveled the world over and formed a part of revolutionary and counterrevolutionary history. Second, outside of the Southern Cone, documentaries informed audiences about the violence of state terrorism, condemned its authors, and mobilized international condemnation of the military junta. From the locus of dictatorship, films made in exile were spurned as subversive and were virtually censored by their inaccessibility to distribution channels. By contrast, in *el exterior* they triggered human rights movements and served as visual testimony and witness for extreme rights violations. Third, documentaries worked to disrupt public debate about the past, specifically those by directors who intended to rupture the political consensus of *olvido* (forgetting) in the technocratic, seamless management of the transition from authoritarianism to democracy.[46] Fourth, documentaries tackled the persistent effects of living with loss in everyday life and its very personal and intimate manifestations, including sexual torture and the psychological effects of captivity. And fifth, documentary films imagined and reconnected communities of Chileans from Santiago to London, recording the unending encounter with loss and its productive use among exile activists.

Because of its constitutive role both nationally and transnationally, I return to documentary film in chapter 5 to analyze culture and exile. I also include other forms of cultural memory that address how the counterrevolution has produced the identities of a second generation of Chileans living in the United States. Through staging memory during protests, founding and running cultural centers, and curating cultural exhibits, Chilean exiles (and their daughters and sons) form a hemispheric bridge of memory. In this chapter I show how the transgenerational transmission of memory of the counterrevolution has shaped the political identities of subsequent generations through key political events, such as Pinochet's arrest and his death, that activate communities of exiles. Located far away both temporally and spatially from its "original" instantiation, the memory symbolics of exile becomes an important form of political and pan-Latina/o identification with other groups who have suffered similar experiences of terror.

At a time when the stakes are exceedingly high for populations living through the aftermath of terror, civil wars, political violence, and the like, it is imperative that scholarship find ways to write about the structuring conditions and agency possibilities, in short the complex personhood, of those that continue to live with these experiences in their bodies, minds, memories, and daily realities. The triangulation between political violence, market objectives, and transitions to democracy—as the rhetoric about the war in Iraq hides and the aftermath of genocide in Guatemala reveals— has indeed become a rule rather than an exception in the current era of globalization. And where democratic transition shows up, as it has in all reaches of the globe, memories of atrocity, though not exclusive, are formulated and cemented through state endeavors. We must tread with caution, and instead of taking policies at face value, work to understand how it is that people perceive, condition, think about, and act upon the legacies of direct violence and its reiteration in ways that directly negotiate the imprint of power.

As these chapters begin to sketch, what was submerged beneath the water and leaking from the refrigerated ship container was not the iceberg's melted runoff but the shadow crevices of disappearances, torture, and forced exile; the bodies and social debris of economic and political restructuring from the nation's counterrevolution against the Allende government, its supporters, and political revolutionary change. In this sense, shadow crevices from the past, alive and dwelling in the present, form a pathway toward the ontology of future possibility.

Searching for Villa Grimaldi

Memory's Democratic Promise

On an unusually warm autumn day in 2002, about three hundred people gathered in front of a makeshift amphitheater at Villa Grimaldi Peace Park.[1] Banners bearing the names of three young people murdered at the site over two decades earlier waved in the light breeze. As people filed into the makeshift amphitheater, volunteers handed them red carnations, a known symbol of mourning and remembrance for those that were disappeared by the dictatorship. Young activists stood chanting political slogans, while relatives of those who were disappeared sat silently in the first row, identifiable by the large black-and-white photos of "missing" loved ones pinned to their chests (fig. 2). Alongside a considerable media presence, the crowd had gathered at the Peace Park for an awards ceremony for lawyer Andrés Aylwin, a champion of human rights and brother of former president Patricio Aylwin. In his acceptance speech, Andrés Aylwin discussed how the event was organized as yet another effort to shed light on the incomplete legal justice for victims and survivors, despite the fact that the transi-

Figure 2.
Viviana Díaz at Villa
Grimaldi Peace Park,
shown with a picture of
her disappeared father,
June 22, 2002. Photo
by Nicole Hayward.

tion to political democracy was, at that point, more than a decade
underway. Those involved in the vision, planning, and architecture of the site spoke of the Peace Park's origins and mission. Others memorialized young militants from the Socialist Party who had
been killed at the Villa Grimaldi concentration camp between 1974
and 1977. Two hundred and twenty-six people are known to have
been assassinated on or disappeared from the property, while more
than four thousand were detained there, most of whom suffered
torture at Villa Grimaldi (fig. 3).

In this chapter I analyze the former concentration camp turned

Figure 3. Sign at the entrance to Villa Grimaldi Peace Park, detailing those held captive there when it was a concentration camp, June 22, 2002. Photo by Nicole Hayward.

memorial that is located on the outskirts of the nation's capital. Villa Grimaldi's transformation is not a story of a conventional heritage site that cements foundational history. The site is more than a symbol of state violence and the recuperation of historical memory, although it is that too. Its grounds, the stories told there, and the cultural and political gatherings that take place at the former concentration camp offer a way to attenuate the persistent after-life of political violence and present the opportunity for building deeper alternative spaces of political democracy. I explore the following questions: How can violence be represented in a way that does not tame memory? What archival and other sources are necessary for uncovering what transpired at the site during authoritarianism? What is the role of a former concentration camp turned memorial park in Chile's process of democratization?

I piece together the story of the Villa Grimaldi concentration camp and its transformation into the Peace Park by studying little-known archives, reviewing an important but scantily known testimonial, and analyzing the architectural elements that have been constructed to imagine the past. I also elaborate on the uses of what may be construed as an alternative public sphere, at least in the nation's imagination in the early transition period. In short, through multiple angles and means, I show how the transformation from concentration camp into a memorial offers a path toward resignifying democracy in the nation.

A question remains: How do we access historical memory, when what is available is incoherent and incomplete, and gestures only toward competing renditions of what occurred at the site? The horrific events at Villa Grimaldi will always be, as Agamben writes about Auschwitz, "singularly opaque when we truly seek to understand them" (1999, 12). Nonetheless, writing about the fragments of history unveils a totalizing historical project. Namely, the shards reveal how Villa Grimaldi was a decisive place of geopolitical extermination in the struggle over the future that the Cold War entailed. What the fragments show is that a complete picture of the past is not a necessary precondition for progress toward a democratic future.

MEMORIAL FORMATIONS

It has become commonplace to consider questions of history and memory as struggles over meaning in the public sphere. Often these forms of historical memory fix and consolidate narratives of national pasts, produce challenges over political power, and work to consolidate and memorialize social and political formations (Walkowitz and Knauer 2004, Crysler 2006, Vidal 1979). One of Villa Grimaldi's challenges to state power is to continually force open the dictatorship's narratives that coded social activists as subversives and terrorists rather than as those in pursuit of justice within a radically unequal society, as a politically Left history might have it. However, Villa Grimaldi is far from a fixed and unchanging project of memorialization that brings forth a conflictive past.[2] Unlike Hiroshima Peace Park and other official sites of atrocity that promote and officialize nationalist discourses, Villa Grimaldi Peace Park's in-progress, unfinished character works against the grain of established renditions. Indeed, as Barbie Zelizer discusses, the terrain of collective violence and its aftermath places multilayered demands upon public forms of cultural memory with high stakes for issues of power, identity, and political affinities (1998, 3).

Public space is often used to memorialize the universal histories of dominant groups and interests, as urban squares and plazas throughout the Americas can confirm, showcasing, reframing, or taming historical subjects for the purposes of constructing a national identity. As architect and historian Dolores Hayden argues, through its use public space can also express important common lived experiences and social identities, in effect producing hybrid forms of cultural citizenship (1995).

Villa Grimaldi Peace Park, in fact, activates such cultural citizenship to deepen the social process of democracy in multiple ways, though they may not be immediately apparent to an outside visitor. First, the park visually displays, however incompletely, a social history of the concentration camp's role in detainment, torture, and disappearance. The site helps fill in the history of the dictatorship's violence with a popular and alternative account of events and practices, details and stories that have been evacuated from the dominant public sphere. Second, the park is a public gathering space where those who were tortured and those who are relatives of the disappeared engage through collective mourning, human rights activism, and the shared experience of sitting with and allowing a space for the ghosts of those that inhabit Villa Grimaldi. As one mother from the Agrupación de Familiares de Detenidos Desaparecidos put it to me, "My son likes it here. It's a calm place where his spirit can rest in peace" (June 2, 2002). Third, the park serves a community and intergenerational function as an open-air cultural center, where theater performances, commemorations, and ceremonies communicate to younger generations of Chileans the history of struggle and counterrevolution. For instance, on the day of the human rights ceremony that I discuss in the opening, dozens of the audience members were under the age of twenty. Many shared how, despite their general knowledge about the dictatorship, through events at the memorial they learned the details, strategies, and excesses of Pinochet's regime. Furthermore, finding out about the cases of the young militants commemorated that day gave them new insights into the era and its effect on their parents' generation and their own. In this way, the gatherings at Villa Grimaldi Peace Park allow for a meaningful reinstatement of the microhistories of political repression, resistance, and its memory.

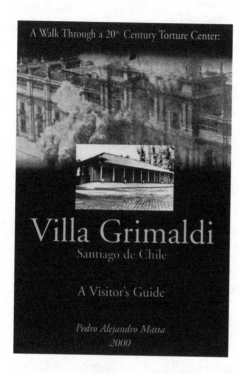

Figure 4. Cover of Pedro Alejandro Matta's 2000 guidebook, featuring "A Walk through a Twentieth-Century Torture Center."

HISTORICAL TENSIONS AND INTENTIONS

In 2002, my tour of Villa Grimaldi Peace Park was of imaginary places, since many of the original structures that were used for torture had been bulldozed by the military.[3] The stately house that is found in photographs in human rights archives, most notably on the cover of the tour manual by Pedro Alejandro Matta, which features "A Walk through a Twentieth-Century Torture Center" (2000) (fig. 4), was absent in the green space before me. Each time I see the cover I ask myself if it is possible to tour atrocity.

In its heyday Villa Grimaldi was a verdant, fruitful villa, built in the architectural style of Spanish colonialism. It boasted fantastic riches, including mosaic pools and European-styled gardens, as the artifacts of the Chilean aristocracy. The main house included marble staircases and several Greek columns supporting its large *fundo* frame. When the furniture and decorations of Villa Grimaldi were up for sale in 1967, the national newspaper *El Mercurio* (November 1967) bragged about the luxuries there. Comparing it to an Italian villa, one article reveals the many virtues of the site: African violets and roses in eternal bloom, the elegance of the "Petit Salon," and the entry's red carpets, carefully weaved through with tiny strands of gold thread. These last items were brought to Chile at the beginning of the 1800s by Don Mateo Toro Zambrano, a "count of the conquest." Archival literature reveals a desire for a retrievable, knowable national past through descriptions of imported goods. These fanciful descriptions helped create a mythology of Villa Grimaldi during the fifties and sixties as a site of wealth, elite pleasures, and exotic landscapes.

The same article in *El Mercurio* scolds the public for not valorizing its history. It reads, "In Chile, as it normally occurs among Latin Americans, these unusual efforts at beauty, tradition, and incalculable historical value go totally unappreciated" (November 1967). It must have been difficult to appreciate what was publicly invisible. The author of the article had intended to write a eulogy for a site of national patrimony, where the country's founding aristocracy had bestowed a jewel on the nation. Reading between the lines of the exaggerated rhetoric shows how Villa Grimaldi was constructed as a national symbol of progress and elegance and class differentiation prior to the military dictatorship that cast detainees as "roto" subversives.[4]

Except for a short period as a restaurant and nightclub, Villa Grimaldi was a place of imitation, where the elite displayed its economic difference from and indifference to Chile's popular classes through a grandeur and opulence it could not sustain. The exact reason for the sale of the property and its conversion to a place for night entertainment is not clear from documents. It is not a coincidence that Villa Grimaldi was purchased by the military in the year of the coup and the year that the Dirección de Inteligencia Nacional, DINA (National Intelligence Directorate), was created. After 1974, Villa Grimaldi was turned into a secret prison for those suspected of working for Allende and the social revolution. The military dictatorship needed to have a place on the outskirts for its efforts to quell "subversives," a place no one would accidentally find. Those who were "in the know" would intentionally arrive there with blindfolded and muffled passengers either slumped in the back seat of DINA's cars or stuffed into the trunk. Villa Grimaldi was the horrendous site of extermination at the hands of DINA's secret police force seeking out-of-the-way places to conduct its dirty work.

DINA agents kidnapped people at their homes, on the streets, at workplaces, at the university, or from other public places and brought them to Villa Grimaldi, mobilizing teams of three of four police officers to blindfold and force them into the back of cars or trucks. The trucks were later turned into instruments of torture, running over the limbs of a prisoner in the courtyard, while other captives were made to watch in disgust, compassion, and powerlessness. Forced voyeurism, similar to what we have seen in places such as Abu Ghraib in the United States' War on Terror, reinscribes the condition of victimhood by further stripping prisoners of agency over their bodies and the bodies of those imprisoned alongside them. Perhaps the primary effect intended by such dramatic performances is that of the captive's shame.

Elspeth Probyn relates Primo Levi's captivity in Auschwitz: "From the shame these inmates of the Lager felt at their own bodies exposed in the gaze of the other, Levi describes the different aspects of shame: 'what the just man experiences at another man's crime; the feeling of guilt that such a crime should exist, that it should have been introduced irrevocably into the world of things that exist, and that his will for good should have proved too weak or null, and should not have availed in defence'" (2005, 160). Shame reminded captives of their abandonment by the state. Scholar Ruth Wilson Gilmore argues, for the U.S. racial state and beyond, that abandonment is the "rigorously coordinated and organized setting aside of people and resources" (2007, 18). Shame, then, is the structure of affect through which state abandonment is performed, a powerful emotion duly mobilized by torturers to diminish and punish prisoners.

As Elaine Scarry elaborated some time ago, torture is the objectification of pain into elements of destruction, such as equipment for electric shocks, rooms that are run-down, and poles to hang captives on (1985). The routine of torture at Villa Grimaldi began at the typewriter, located at entry points to the prison as an artifact of documentation that offers the farce of confessions. Elements were carefully planned and then orchestrated to produce the extreme matrix of power at the concentration camp, designed to create maximum fear in a wider populace. If accounts of how Villa Grimaldi was organized leaked from the confines of the prison, it was even better, because the mere threat of entering a place like Villa Grimaldi gave the state's dirty work an omnipresence in the nation. Although archival documents declare Villa Grimaldi's absence, as I soon detail, its existence was the dictatorship's most broadcast national secret. This scenario is not unlike

Figure 5. The *parrilla* (grill), a torture device, drawn by Miguel Lawner, 1976. From Lawner, *Isla Dawson, Ritoque, Tres Álamos . . .: La vida a pesar de todo* (Santiago: Lom Ediciones, 2003).

the visual pervasiveness of torture practices at Abu Ghraib, despite the ongoing official denial.[5] Thus, fear through the illogic of contradiction forms a core tactic and strategy of social containment.

Arriving prisoners would circulate between a routine of torture practices, where each specialized technique had a geographically specific site at the camp. One of the most massively used forms of torture was the *parrilla* (grill) (fig. 5), practiced in a barren room with only an "iron bedstead, a desk with a tape recorder, a chair, and an electric shock device" (Scarry 1985, 12). The prisoner was made to unclothe and was tied to the bedstead, sometimes upside down, while shock devices were tied or inserted into their genitals and other parts of the body. A session could not last beyond two or three hours, for the body does not withstand more (ibid.). When the torture was physically unbearable and produced heart attacks, the inability to breathe, and so on, doctors would help revive the patient to the point of regaining consciousness so the session could resume at that time or a later date.[6] Names like "the dove," "the wet submarine," and "the perch" were given to forms of torture, crudely referring to the position of captives who were hung from their wrists or dunked in cold water in an old oil barrel for minutes on end. The *pau de arara* (parrot's perch), where a person was forced to squat and hold their knees while a pole was passed between their arms and legs to hang them upside down, was a technique of torture imported from Brazil.[7]

As in other concentration camps that sprung up in Chile, torture at Villa Grimaldi was employed as a primary form of punishment, meted out for the extraction of information. Its use on the bodies of revolutionaries was a method to bludgeon the broad coalition of the political Left, which included the Movimiento de Izquierda Revolucionaria, MIR (Revolutionary Left Movement), the armed guerrilla and militant political movement. Torture was employed as a means to erase the memory of the mass social movement. In the 1970s, these activists and revolutionaries had heterogeneous visions of globalization, which included a socialist dream that would have to be fought for against an entrenched national elite with global capitalist corporate linkages. In other words, at Villa Grimaldi there was a struggle over social ideas, economic programs, and political possibilities wherein the bodies of male and female revolutionaries were made to pay for trespassing power and privilege. Moreover, as a spatial construction and torture experiment, Villa Grimaldi was an expression of the backlash against social movements and mass organization in Latin

America. It was also the site of the transformation of torture in the Americas, where experimental torture on a case-by-case basis—for instance, the pulling of teeth and nails—was replaced by systematic torture practices (Colectivo de Arte 2001).

Villa Grimaldi does and does not exist, depending on where you look for it. On March 20, 1976, the official record and voice of the nation *El Mercurio* claimed that "Villa Grimaldi is a place where people are only interrogated when they are detained, and soon after are given liberty."[8] It was described as merely a place of "transit" for the prisoner where "normal conditions are practiced, without physical pressure" (ibid.). State officials denied its existence as a site of interrogation and extermination. In June 1977 a similar message came from the Ministry of Interior, presumably the quarters where all detained and arrested persons were to be processed: "There does not exist, nor has there existed a detention camp by the name of Villa Grimaldi." The government letter, marked confidential, was signed César Raúl Benavides Escobar, then minister of the interior.

Searching beyond the official story, there are testimonials and tour guides that pinpoint exactly when and why Villa Grimaldi existed. Villa Grimaldi is a site of cultural memory that challenges what is known about state terror. It is a geographically marginal site that embodies the stories of those who were captive there, but in the many official archival sources, it never existed as a concentration camp. Its existence is ephemeral and has to pass through testimonies and other forms of representation to be recognized as the material historical experiment of torture and terror that it was. Through ethnography and testimonials, I show the tension in the veracity of these stories about the nation's violent past and suggest its important location within efforts to acknowledge atrocity, offering a possibility for democratic reshaping through historical witness.

TOURING ATROCITY IN MEMORY'S ABSENCE

It was a cold day in June 2002 in Santiago, with mist hanging over the Peace Park. I was the sole visitor that day. An older woman sat warming herself by a teakettle in a poorly insulated trailer office and offered me a cup of tea to break the chill of winter. She guided me across the park to our first destination: a small *maqueta*, or architectural model, of the site as it stood before its destruction. I had been struck by the openness of the park, the lack of buildings in the enormous lot full of plants and trees. The archive had not prepared me for an outdoor tour that, at a glance, contained no spaces of horror that one might enter. The model provided an important mental picture, where buildings, dark cells, and torture devices emerged in the imagination, replacing the physical presence of open space. Only later did I realize that open space signified erasure. If there is nothing for the mind to grasp, then there is no evidence of history—or is there? What are the traces of history that one follows for evidence of social reality? What forms of knowing emerge from remains that unhinge the primacy of empirical knowledge?

The Villa Grimaldi concentration camp was the exception to other sites of clandestine power (Londres 38, José Domingo Cañas, the Discothèque, the Venda Sexy), salvaged and preserved by a group of concerned activists and witnesses, many of whom had been former prisoners at the site. As the locus of atrocities, it was on the verge of extinction when a group of activists intervened to acquire the property. In fact, at the point of their intervention, architectural plans for modern condominiums had been approved, and the land was in the process of being cleared (Richard 2001, 10–13). After the property was turned over to the activists, the Corporación Parque por la Paz (Peace Park Committee) made its central mission that of preserving historical memory as an emblem of the systems of state terror. As the trilingual Web site details, the objectives of the Peace Park Committee are "[t]o preserve the history and memory of Villa Grimaldi and other detention and torture centers, their facilities and symbolic places" and "to spread and encourage Human Rights awareness."[9] In an earlier document, the committee's public objective was more complexly stated, positioning Villa Grimaldi as "a very important symbolic and historical effort that congregates, makes alive, condemns and resignifies the problem of violations and justice for all prisoners" (Art Collective 2001). In both statements the language of global human rights discourse is present, where an international human rights community gives credence to the work of preservation and transmission of historical memory of the concentration camp.

Touring Villa Grimaldi with my guide allowed me to begin to recognize the social and spatial organization of terror and survival. There were stories here. As she told me, somewhere between 1976 and 1977, the mosaic-tiled swimming pool, emptied of its cool water, was transformed into a receptacle to hide malnourished and abused prisoners by a military eager to deny Villa Grimaldi as a concentration camp. While Red Cross inspectors were taken to specific parts of the property, prisoners had their mouths taped shut and were taken at gunpoint to the large pool, then packed like sardines into its dry depths (June 10, 2002). Even on the large tract of land that was Villa Grimaldi, it is hard to imag-

Figure 6. The *perreras* (kennels), small drawers used as a form of torture, drawn by Miguel Lawner, 1976. From Lawner, *Isla Dawson, Ritoque, Tres Álamos . . .: La vida a pesar de todo* (Santiago: Lom Ediciones, 2003).

ine how dozens of prisoners could pass unnoticed by human rights investigators.

When I returned in 2005 I visited the far northeastern corner of the property, where a new building had been reconstructed to resemble a torture site called the Tower. The multitiered fifty-foot oak building contains replicas of a series of torture spots, including isolation cells that are smaller than seven feet by three feet, with less space than the closets of solitary confinement (*las perreras*, or kennels) that had been used for prisoners who did not "collaborate enough" (Matta 2000, 13–14) (fig. 6). My guide emphasized several times that it was difficult to know what happened at the Tower, as there were no survivors. The Tower had been recon-

Figure 7. Example of the tiles used to mark the areas where prisoners were tortured. The translation of this tile reads, "Former parking lot. Place where cars were used for torture." Villa Grimaldi Peace Park, June 22, 2002. Photo by Nicole Hayward.

structed to produce the simulacrum of terror, but the experiential effect was uneven. The smell and look of the wood was new and, during the times I visited, several people climbed playfully to the various rooms that housed the cells, looking out of windows to catch a view of the surrounding Andes. Some visitors have since told me that climbing into the oak tower and then into the very small cells was for them a compelling experience that produced empathy for captives. When I visited, a group of young men was talking about how they could never imagine squeezing into such small confines, but these moments of identification were overshadowed by a couple's preoccupation with taking photographs of the surrounding mountains.

In many places, only signs made of small bricks, foundation, and ceramic mosaic exist as aesthetic indications of what transpired (fig. 7). Some of these signs mark the specific use of the

areas where torture took place; others indicate the area's approximate size. Indeed, through the architectural fixtures and re-creations of the site, the immense proportions of pain and suffering
are impossible to imagine, at least without knowing the social history narrated through individual stories of captivity.

ENCOUNTERING CARMEN ROJAS

In an offhand manner, my guide showed me *Recuerdos de una Mirista* (Memories of an MIR Member) by Carmen Rojas, a small
book with a black and red cover whose testimony about the place
of terror filled what was still open space in my search. In the same
way that the docent's words, Matta's guidebook, and the small
model of Villa Grimaldi provided a way to find out more about
what happened, my encounter with Carmen Rojas's testimony unsettling account gave gendered voice to what I had known of the
ontology of captivity and torture at Villa Grimaldi.

There are two parallel texts in *Recuerdos de una Mirista*, which
together provide a compelling testimony of memory on the margins of the democratic transition, stories that may serve to intrude
on the erasure of female revolutionary history. First there is a narration of captivity that moves in Rojas's internal world of nightmares. This narrative of circularity and self-reflexivity recounts
the trauma of torture through images, silences, screams, blindness, voices, and visions. There is also an external text that is a
political narrative full of longing, references, and analysis of the
revolutionary crisis of MIR during the early and most violent
phase of the dictatorship. Rojas's narrative is astounding, not
merely as a chronicle and testimonial (a primary document that
makes no claims to universal experience) but also as a deeply mov-

ing psychological, social, affective, and political journey through a woman's life in complex and dangerous times.[10] I was disturbed by the work, which seemed to beckon forward the voices of the dead and their lived encounters as political prisoners.

As Rojas's testimonial evidences, the violence at Villa Grimaldi, as at other concentration camps, reproduced the gender hierarchies and social practices of the wider Chilean society by using sexual torture as a mechanism of terror. Male torturers threatened women prisoners with rape and humiliated them on the basis of their bodily functions. Torture is the expression of "intimate bonds between the male military captor and the sometimes female captive, bonds that intertwine political and sexual repression" (Gordon 2007, 67).[11] Building on this insight, it seems that by entangling political and sexual repression, torture disarticulated the political Left and the collective agency of its gendered social actors. That is, torture was as much about emasculating male subjects through exerting control over their bodies as it was about humiliating female revolutionaries, punishing their trespassing of a patriarchal status quo.[12]

Carmen Rojas was a prisoner at Villa Grimaldi, knowing the place through the terror of her body and experiencing the insatiable "ceremony of torture" at the hands of one of the most feared men in the history of the nation. Romo was a notorious agent of DINA who tortured her and countless others, especially targeting female prisoners with specialized sadistic techniques. In fact, Romo was an emblematic male prototype of the particular historical juncture, a protagonist of the dictatorship and the counterrevolution against Allende's Chilean road to socialism.

For Rojas in the invisible confines of Villa Grimaldi, Romo was a malignant and omnipresent character with unimaginable power over her body. As described in Rojas's book, Romo repeatedly threatens her verbally, saying, "Do you know where you are? You're in the DINA. . . . Are you scared?" In the face of his fear tactics and sheer destructive capacity, Rojas's silence becomes a form of agency that mediates his inability to control all of her bodily functions, even while the exercise of power in the concentration camp induces and reproduces patriarchal quests for total control. In one account, she is forced to urinate in front of her torturer for fear that she will not get a chance to relieve herself later. In another moment in the book, Rojas describes how Romo makes her undress and remove a strip of colored cloth from her wrist (a gift that calmed her). With the help of other male torturers, Romo straps Rojas to the *parrilla*, and while they electrocute her they laugh at the menstrual blood that drips down her legs (ca. 1981, 24). In such instances, the mobilization of shame, particularly shame of the female body controlled by male power, is a quintessential condition of the captive experience. In this case the essential definition of shame as "an exposure of the intimacies of selves in public," as Elspeth Probyn tells us, is literalized through the nude female body made to publicize the individualization of private bodily functions. The state, through its secret agents, trafficked in the affect of shame and the production of pain, maintaining its gender power hierarchies in these ways. Even so, a retreat to interiority, a subject I discuss in more detail in the next chapter, offered spaces for (in this case) female agency, disabling the state's fantasy of total control and concomitantly the total destruction of the prisoner's subjectivity.[13] Silence was used as a form of resistance but also as a form of self-preservation, where the retreat to interior landscapes was another form of living through the condition of imprisonment.

Like other political prisoners, Rojas was committed to the seemingly impossible objective of not revealing her companions' whereabouts or other information about them. As she remembers, "I was obsessed with having a coherent story to tell without contradicting myself. . . . I tried to make up imaginary beings, invent names and circumstances, but I couldn't remember them even for short periods" (C. Rojas ca. 1981, 33). Her fear of failing to keep to her story is common among prisoners, who would often rather be killed than deceive their *compañero/as*.[14] Unlike Luz Arce, another female captive who did break down, Rojas was able to defend herself through conviction and silence rather than disclose relevant knowledge of militants and militant activity. As Rojas put it, "Not to speak! Not to speak was the objective. Skinny wouldn't do it, Eduardo wouldn't either. To speak was worse than to die" (C. Rojas ca. 1981, 17). Rojas, however, should not be passively regarded as heroic for the fact that she did not speak during, as she calls it, the "inacabable ceremonia de la tortura" (never-ending ritual of torture) (ibid., 25). A simple distinction between "traitor" and "non-traitor" discounts the unbearable psychological torture endured by both male and women prisoners, and the additional sexual torture endured mostly by female captives. Thus, in some ways the desire to not be broken down loses meaning in front of sheer violence, pain, and the objectification of the body as a site of state brutality. Extreme conditions of violence often erase the possibility of volition and will. And there are consequences of being forced to tell. Luz Arce, for instance, spent years of banishment from political communities of survivors because of her revelations to the DINA.

While the oppression of female and male prisoners is a central thread in the text, Rojas also weaves another story, one that contradicts the framework of domination and total submission at Villa Grimaldi. Although she forced herself at all costs to remain silent as prisoner, in print she speaks with clarity and precision about the position of MIR at that moment. This political voice remains committed to social ideals and carefully articulates tactics, strategies, and their consequences under an authoritarian regime. She wonders about the possibility of resistance, "of not allowing oneself to be defeated by an enemy, of resisting when that is the only alternative" (ca. 1981, 37–38). Despite the fact that defeat of the revolutionary party seemed imminent, the MIR continued to function. The story of the resistance of MIR attests to the other historical paths not taken on the road to dictatorship violence and economic neoliberalism.

Rojas insists on answers for a particular historical period, both in Chile and around the world. More specifically, she tries to understand the limits of the revolutionary movement she embraces, by analyzing the class structure of the MIR and the political interpretations of the time. She asks if the vision is inherently restricted, if MIR's connection to its mass base is adequate, and if there is sufficient leadership to direct the political struggle before them. Moreover, she questions MIR's quest for basic survival: "Is this where things should be going? No? Then, how can we respond and make changes?" (ibid., 59). In one striking example of the historical, intellectual, and activist connections she makes, Rojas analyzes the relationship between Chilean and other global political struggles. Referring to the exiles of the dictatorship, Rojas says, "That group of young people and leaders came out of the struggles that were happening not only in Chile, but also in various countries within Latin America, in Asia, in Africa, and in all the places where there was a struggle for more freedom and less hypocrisy. They were part of a generation that felt, in their own bodies, the struggle of Vietnam, and that vibrated during the anti-imperialist marches. They found their 'mestizo' and American roots, and thought deeply about the terms of dependence in order to know why and with whom they struggled" (ibid., 59).

Perhaps it is not surprising that Rojas, as a political prisoner, would contextualize her experiences within Villa Grimaldi, namely by connecting the global histories of anti-imperialist struggles. At the same time, her testimonial includes an extraordinary range of historical knowledge and a broad understanding of resistance movements, interrupting the paradigm of the male figure in Latin America as the quintessential revolutionary subject.[15] She also complicates testimonies of victimhood that are produced for Western consumption, which leave revolutionary subjectivity and its reading as background to the narrative.[16] In sum, Rojas is not only a victim of masculine power but an active subject in the struggle for social liberation, a female figure of the revolutionary Left in Latin America. Undeniably, there is a hidden history at Villa Grimaldi, of MIR and its resistance told through a tortured, blindfolded, and silenced militant, wanted by the state for her knowledge and political involvement. Rojas represents, to rephrase Che Guevara's classic terminology, the "new woman," a political subject within a context of violence where men and masculinities were often positioned at the epicenter of the revolutionary quake. Her narrative attends to the nuanced and embodied experiences of Villa Grimaldi, unwittingly raising the question of female agency and resistance in an arena where victimhood may otherwise appear as the only plausible form of identification. What were the social interactions among Villa Grimaldi's prisoners, including their solidarity, networks, and mechanisms of survival? Although these do not emerge entirely in the text, Rojas implies that organized resistance existed through a network of messages, female solidarity in the prisons, and small acts of collective defiance.

In previous sections I have discussed the routine of terror that took place at Villa Grimaldi, although it is not always reflected in the current physicality of the public memorial. The subject positions of *victims* and *survivors* emerge strongly in the stories that are told about the place, in part as a way to mark the fact of these occurrences. For many years, Pinochet supporters denied the grave atrocities that took place at Villa Grimaldi and other such concentration camps, as well as the media censorship about such truths. Thus, those who suffered political violence were made to tell their stories in exacting detail and to shoulder the burden of evidence to prove torture or a disappearance. Touring Villa Grimaldi can enhance this human rights perspective, while the process of creating awareness about the violence carried out on bodies can diminish the perception of the modes of resistance and social agency that persisted, despite impossible conditions. Rojas's testimonial revises the story of victimhood by revealing the political project of MIR, illuminating the particular gendered experience of captivity, and gesturing toward an organized system of survival between prisoners. Without this information, the Peace Park memorial casts victims and survivors within a limited frame. In this sense, the rhetoric of human rights that seizes upon fixed categories may ignore and thereby erase multiple social and political identities, especially those as protagonists of revolutionary history, even if ultimately defeated as a social movement by the military state.[17]

Rojas's testimony of her captivity in Villa Grimaldi and other concentration camps documented the wide network of activists involved in a new social project for the nation. These activists were tortured and disappeared at places like Villa Grimaldi, first to subdue socialism and later to impose free market principles. Like Guillermo Núñez's artistic production, which I detail in the next chapter, Carmen Rojas's story and testimonial illustrate how Chile's "economic success"[18] was made through the devastation of a social body with particular political identities and social dreams.[19]

PEACE PARK ARCHITECTURE

Robin Wagner-Pacifici and Barry Schwartz describe how "memorial devices are not self-created; they are conceived and built by those who wish to bring to consciousness the events and people that others are more inclined to forget. To understand memorial making in this way is to understand it as a construction process wherein competing 'moral entrepreneurs' seek public arenas and support for their interpretations of the past. These interpretations are embodied in the memorial's symbolic structure" (2002, 211–12). By March 22, 1997, the day the Peace Park was inaugurated, Villa Grimaldi had been thoroughly transformed by the vision of a group of artists and architects. Because the military and, later, developers had bulldozed most of the physical evidence of state terror, architects and artists had few elements with which to design a Peace Park that was faithful to its origins. Unlike former concentration camps that display a vast store of objects as material evidence of atrocity (for instance, the piles of worn shoes at Auschwitz), at Villa Grimaldi there were few such remnants.[20] Thus, the design of the Peace Park was accomplished through a communal cultural effort to re-imagine and aesthetically represent the concentration camp as an effort to create awareness in the nation and beyond.

The most notable representational element in the park is an "X" that converges in the middle of the terrain to symbolize freedom and purification. As an organizational map of the space, the X divides the park into four corners. At the center lies a series of concentric circles that form a water fountain, which is also a symbol of purification. One branch of the X leads to the Tower and another to prison cells, creating a path between different torture sites. The other two branches lead to the entrance of the park and to the Wall of Names memorial area. Initially, I read the X as a cross (albeit with a short leg, as in the symbol for addition). The cross makes an important historical reference, one that international visitors might perceive as religious, but which operates within Chile's history of dictatorship and resistance. Meaningfully, the cross summons the slogan "Nunca +," meaning "Never again" or "No More," that was popularly used by the human rights movement during the military dictatorship (Santa Cruz 1999, 45). This resonant symbol, originally designed by artist Lotty Rosenfeld, was utilized by a growing human rights movement in Chile in need of a quick way to register opposition in urban areas under surveillance. For those with knowledge and experience of this history, the symbolism would immediately register, since this became a signature of the anti-Pinochet, pre-referendum movement of 1988.

By far the most important bridge to the memory of those who suffered in Villa Grimaldi is the Muro de los Nombres, or Wall of Names. This is the centerpiece of the architectural additions, although it is located at the far end of the Peace Park, near a rose garden and behind the burnt tree in recovery where priests sometimes hold remembrance ceremonies for the disappeared. A few concrete steps lead down toward the large copper wall at the back of the memorial site, a placement that enhances a sentiment of privacy and reverence for those whose legal names, dates of birth, and dates of death (if known) are etched onto the thick surface. As the wall itself indicates, those listed were *detenidos desapareci-dos*, prisoners who were detained at Villa Grimaldi between 1974–1977 and then disappeared by the military; Villa Grimaldi was the last site of their known whereabouts. This place is where relatives of the disappeared quietly talk to, cry for, and otherwise communicate with the ghosts of their loved ones. Some go to remember their own encounter with torture and captivity.

As historian Mario Aguilar suggests, the open character of the list on the Wall of Names, where names are added when stories are made complete, is an important reflection of the present struggle over locating those who were disappeared. The fact that names are continually added illustrates the unending saga of family members of the disappeared, many who have yet to piece together the details of the assassination of loved ones (1999, 84). The wall is also a reflection of the unfinished business and legacy of state terror. The memorial's open quality brings into relief the state narrative of closure over the past. If spaces on the memorial mean that missing bodies have yet to be located, can the memory of state violence be reconciled? In many ways, the material absences of the missing emphasize the legal and emotional incompleteness of political democracy and the democratic transition.

A documentary film by Germán Liñeros called *El Muro de los Nombres* (Wall of Names) explains how the memorial was commissioned (2000). Sculptor Paula Rubio and won the public contest for the site-specific work. As one member of the Peace Park Committee describes in the short film, "the chosen work lent itself to meditation, especially so that people don't pass through quickly and indifferently alongside a wall, reading through the names at the same time. Also, [they created] a small theater where one can sit, reflect, think, and evoke." Another member enters the frame and adds, "We didn't want it to be cold, like the one at the cemetery, where we had to throw red carnations from afar. [The artists] wanted us to be able to sit there, those of us who are family members of the disappeared." The reference to the General Cemetery Memorial for the Disappeared as "cold" is often heard from relatives of the disappeared: "a cold memorial that sits above the viewer," and "a memorial of the state" (pers. comm., January–June 2002). The emphasis on a place to sit down directly in front of the wall is critical to understanding the different affective space this memorial produces as a place of contemplation with no barriers, in private, in solace. In contrast, at the General Cemetery Memorial visitors are forced to stand back or stroll through the plaza at some distance from the main memorial. Even so, people are able to place personal shrines in the crevices of the large boulders at the bottom of the wall, although as visitors grow older, it becomes more difficult for them to sit near the wall on the giant boulders.[21]

As a memory symbolic the Peace Park occupies a different imaginary in the nation, even if both memorials are now part of regular tours of atrocity and memory. Although the Peace Park was realized in part through state resources, the memorial at the General Cemetery was built exclusively with government funds and backing from the highest levels. In fact, the memorial was a symbolic effort by the early transition government to integrate the then strong and visible human rights movement. According to AFDD president Viviana Díaz, members of the human rights community negotiated with transition president Patricio Aylwin,

Figure 8. The Muro de los Nombres (Wall of Names). Villa Grimaldi
Peace Park, January 5, 2005. Photo by author.

and his minister of interior ultimately made an agreement with
the AFDD about the project, with uneven results (interview with
the author, April 19, 2002).[22] At this early moment in the transition, a memorial to the disappeared was a revealing symbolic gesture of reintegration into the nation for those who had borne the
burden of state terror. The high profile of the memorial at the
cemetery gives it a different historical constitution and meaning
than the Wall of Names at Villa Grimaldi. When sculptor Paula
Rubio is interviewed in *El Muro de los Nombres*, she focuses on the
unearthing of memory that the Wall of Names attempts to represent. Fossil-like figures are attached to the wall's surface, which
for her symbolize the fossilized forms of the past that are "represented and rescued in the present through this wall" (fig.8).

More recently, a Memory Room was added to the physical structures of the Park, where a small selection of prisoners' photos and their personal items are displayed (fig. 9). Black and white photographs, pieces of people's lives, childhood toys, journal entries, and scraps of paper with scribbles provide a more intimate portrait of the lives that were made to disappear at Villa Grimaldi. The Memory Room is indeed a location where memories dwell, a compelling location of memory's lack rather than its reinscription, since the room provokes memories that never existed for the majority of visitors. Indeed, this other memory emerges right at the doorway, in the stares of those who once passed through Villa Grimaldi—a memory beyond the legal identification of names, beyond the "experiential" architecture. Suddenly, one is confronted with the inhabitance of things and ideas, faces and eyes that form a memoryscape against the tide of forgetting.

This constellation of elements structures the Peace Park as a place of solace, commemoration, and mourning. Its components (with the exception of the Memory Room) bracket the experiences at Villa Grimaldi as those of trauma, loss, and victimhood. That is, rather than highlight the national issue of domination, resistance, revolution, and counterrevolution that was at stake at Villa Grimaldi, the architectural elements of the park are framed in this limited understanding of the multifaceted history that the place represents, presenting an important, albeit ultimately limited, view of the past. Does memorializing necessarily imply taming memory and co-opting the act of resistance?

Cultural scholar Lisa Yoneyama explores how the constitution and planning of public space in Hiroshima in the aftermath of the atom bomb has tamed memories of the violence and obliteration. The reworking of spaces to reveal a "bright and cheerful

Figure 9. "Fragments of a Life," a display in the Memory Room. Villa Grimaldi Peace Park, January 5, 2005. Photo by author.

peace" rather than exhibit the "'dark' memories of war and the bomb"—especially in the context of corporate events, tourism, and development projects—ends up taming the city's history of decimation (1999, 44). In the case of Villa Grimaldi, the narrative of peace is present, but peace is defined in terms of solace rather than of new national beginnings.

One of the early objectives of the Peace Park was to create a "place of memory where so much of Chilean history had taken place. . . . Later, local organizations based in Peñalolén pushed for the property to be given to a corporation that would build a park for peace (Parque por la Paz de Villa Grimaldi). Such an idea followed the wish of organizations that the park would constitute a symbolic memento against torture" (Aguilar 2003, 13). Of course, representing torture in the absence of buildings and architectural spaces used for such purposes is a tricky endeavor. Thus, reconstructed torture sites and open space have been used as symbolic formats for the complexity of representing torture. This explains, for instance, the park's open and spacious constitution and the particular arrangement of spaces of reflection at the site, such as the rose garden, the Wall of Names, and various green areas. Even so, the Peace Park Committee's expressive definition of human rights imagines that open space, art, and memorial sites function to promote contemplation and comprehension alongside fixtures of state terror such as torture cells. True to the park's stated objective, the committee mobilizes the term *human rights* as a way to capture international attention for this history. The Peace Park does work as a gathering place to remember individual and collective loss, reflected in architectural elements that produce such opportunities.

Prior to the architectural reconstructions in the park, cultural critic Nelly Richard had arrived at a different conclusion, describing how a visitor to the Peace Park is overwhelmed with the sensation of openness, which seems to belie the suffocating enclosure that political prisoners experienced. In this context, she asks, "What relationship is created between the mental cavities that were perforated with fear, the holes and breakages within the [prisoner's] consciousness that made its way through the labyrinth of craziness of a past in cells, and this diagram and current system of regular lines and proportions that offer the visitor an outing of order and cleanliness?" (2001, 12). Of course, Richard knew it was not the architects' plans but the military's bulldozers that destroyed the evidence of the Villa Grimaldi concentration camp. Her provocation thus demands that we wrestle with the representational issues of the history of captivity—issues that are not easily summoned or dismissed through a liberal human rights agenda, which, in the case of Villa Grimaldi, may tend toward diminishing the historical memory of resisting terror.

Richard sees the cross shape that meets at the center of the park as one of several systematic attempts to represent the site in terms of peace, rather than highlighting its history of resistance, as Rojas's story does, by introducing more destabilizing representational elements. Even adding the name of Peace Park to Villa Grimaldi suggests a less radical confrontation with the place's history of violence and terror. Moreover, the smooth surface of the tall glass structure that provides illumination for nighttime cultural activities in the park might aesthetically detract from an imaginary centered on the dirty and sadistic quality of terror carried out in the place.

The open space and new construction flattens the possibility for an experience of horror, since strolling across the lawns can feel like an escape from the city. The notion of escape in fact evokes at least three ontological and temporal configurations: contemplation of terror by visitors in its aftermath, the death and thereby escape of prisoners from torture, and the impossibility of escape by captive prisoners. An entryway that one must imagine, walls that tumbled, closets and towers that were bulldozed—some of which were reconstructed and smell new—and a tree that is slowly recovering from a fire that attempted to erase all evidence cannot capture the confinement, the fear, the captivity of thousands, or the tsunami of pain and violence produced for thousands more. Does the Peace Park obstruct the memory of atrocity? Is the architectural purpose to provide a site of peace and mourning for victims and their families, where spirits and memories can be quelled through open space and restful gardens?

Perhaps one response to these questions lies in the multiple uses of the Peace Park. Rather than analyzing the park as solely an architectural site, to be scrutinized by only its symbolic elements, I have chosen to include the voices of Carmen Rojas, other activists who use the Peace Park for social gatherings, and my guide. These voices and narratives deepen the social meaning of the Peace Park, as forms of memory that force a different reconstruction of historical memory in the nation. At Villa Grimaldi Peace Park, architecture and design facilitate the purpose of retrieving a past of collective violence and its afterlife. Moreover, the historical connection between social actors, events, and experience emerges only through gatherings of human rights activists, theater, memorial ceremonies, and tours. Indeed, despite the complexities of representation and memory, the Peace Park constructs an alternative public sphere that is enhanced and made salient through spaces of reflection and architectural design.

VILLA GRIMALDI is an unusual case for the many nations in the region that endured authoritarian regimes, because although it was bulldozed and suffered fires, the site was preserved and reconstructed rather than altogether destroyed. As such, its charter can be burdened with endless demands to address the past in a meaningful way that does not flatten catastrophe. Like sites that now have greater public recognition in the nation, including the Memorial for the Disappeared at the General Cemetery in Santiago, Villa Grimaldi exists only because of the work of a group of concerned activists and former prisoners. The two goals of representing brutal history and creating a space of rest must work together to promote cultural activities that stir imaginations and social activism about terror, death, and survival.

By bringing forth the memories of Villa Grimaldi, including the subjectivities of violent rupture and their persistent hold over many, one opens the door to the possibilities for democracy—not as a flat and elitist ideal but as a complex form of social and political organization that is attuned to the affective, physical, psychological, material, and spiritual well-being of a population. Nelly Richard poses the question, "What memory map is drawn from the fractured stones and gardens of Villa Grimaldi?" (2001, 11). By looking at Villa Grimaldi's history we get a better picture of how economic neoliberalism was forced upon a population through torture and terror. The Peace Park (on the margins of Santiago and of the historical record) sheds light on the dictatorship and its enduring impact, as well as the neoliberal remaking of the nation. It shows how the social groups and identities produced by dictatorship (relatives of the disappeared, survivors, revolutionaries, and so on) exercise a particular form of cultural citizenship, one that is imbricated with the history of authoritarian brutality.

The place condenses historical meaning about how the neoliberal revolution was won in Chile and about the underside of

Chile's entrance into market-driven globalization, namely its punishing of revolutionary activity and of the gendered bodies who carried it out. Carmen Rojas's narrative refuses a reductionist account of victimization by state violence by forcing us to reckon with the complexity of female revolutionary subjectivity prior to and during captivity. Fortunately, this refusal also allows us to take one step closer to the complex memoryscape of terror. The Peace Park and Carmen Rojas's narrative are important remains of the socialist defeat of the 1970s and the high human cost of the rapid turn toward market practices.

The difficult and unsettling memories of Villa Grimaldi can be positioned within social, political, and symbolic fields of power and history. Perhaps such excesses cannot be monumentalized in places themselves, but rather in the passage through places—in a journey through the narration of Carmen Rojas, through the transmissions of human rights activists, through the stories of survivors, and through the careful, detailed explanations of tour guides. In fact, Villa Grimaldi is not a place that is easily reached or understood. And I do not mean to settle its meaning here, for surely the memory tours now offered by tourist companies in Chile reveal that at least in the international sphere, and perhaps also within the country, the possible move from invisibility to hypervisibility as a tourist destination could again give new meaning to Villa Grimaldi's place in the historical record. The place of memory's signification indeterminately continues.

For me, the search began as a missing piece in the archive, continued along Tobalaba Avenue in public buses and taxis, retreated in the open space of the Peace Park, and descended into the terror imaginary of testimonial literature. After a long period of submersion it reappeared in the architectural elements of the Park. It was and continues to be a circular and spiraling search that evokes the past, the making of identities, and the social activity of the present. If you look for it you will find both absence of memory and its meaningful social recuperation at Villa Grimaldi Peace Park.

Making Torture Visible

*The Art of Guillermo Núñez
in Chile's Transition*

Like the nearby former concentration camp Villa Grimaldi, Guillermo Núñez's home was hard to find. Núñez lives at the base of the Andes in Macul,[1] a community on the outer edge of Santiago that was once far removed from the city but is now quickly filling up with condominiums and commercial vineyards. Núñez shares his modest adobe house with literary and cultural critic Soledad Bianchi. In many ways, his home and land can be seen as a symbol of resistance to the surrounding condominium developments with street upon street of sameness, an observation that Núñez also proffered. Núñez's art studio, a modernist structure that allows light to flood through a series of small windows, is located at the end of a short path leading from the rear entrance of his house; tacked up on walls and scattered across long carpenter tables was artwork in various stages. Themes of torture were obvious at first sight, visual representations of the emotional, psy-

Figure 10. Painter Guillermo Núñez at his home
in Macul, Chile, March 29, 2002. Photo by author.

chic, and physical body in pain under abnormal conditions of
duress and destruction by the hand of state power (Scarry 1985).[2]

As a survivor of torture who was held captive and blindfolded
for five months during Pinochet's regime, Guillermo Núñez (fig.
10) has a critical and instructive take on the period of the transition to democracy, which has been characterized by the continu-
ation of the military regime's economic liberalization policies. It

is no coincidence that Núñez's home space, land, and artscape *feel* antithetical to the commodity culture and real estate trends in the nation, for these economic trends were accomplished, constructed, and reconciled through repression of the individual and collective body, and repression of its social dreams. The tortured body cannot be separated from the neoliberal turn in the nation, since it was through severe punishment that the military state imposed its multifold project of "fiscal discipline," free trade, flexibilization of labor, privatization of state enterprises, and reentrance into global capitalist economic structures.[3]

In this chapter, primarily through Núñez's visual work, I show how the tortured body and its representation force open a confrontation with the social costs of the oft-touted economic "Chilean miracle."[4] A focus on underpaid workers, increasing income gaps, social inequality, policy measures, weakened unions, and a bleak environmental picture reveals the failures of the neoliberal economic model (Winn 2004, Barrera 1998, Collins and Lear 1995, Petras and Leiva 1994). The exploitation of the rural female labor force and of other workers, the criminalization of indigenous social movements, and xenophobia, especially toward immigrants from Peru, are only a few examples of the structures of exclusion that the economic model has seized upon and produced in the nation. Another way to think about the high social costs of the economic model is through history and culture, especially the political work of torture, its expression and experience, and the incommensurable rift that it caused.

The explicit aim of torture was to tame the tidal wave of mobilizations that had culminated in the formation of Unidad Popular, the coalition that brought Allende to power—to tame its promise, its memory. Within the ideological framing of the Cold

War and U.S. geopolitics in the region, secret agents used torture as the means to extract information from militants and others they labeled subversives and terrorists. Religion scholar William Cavanaugh identifies this method as "not simply a contest over the visible, physical body; it is better understood as a contest over the social *imagination*, in which bodies are the battleground" (1998, 58; italics in the original).[5] As would be repeated elsewhere in Latin America, the military state promoted the discourse of civil war as a means to justify human rights violations of civilians, even though the vast majority of the population was unarmed. Especially during the early to mid 1970s, torture punished revolutionary thought and its project, destroying what had become an increasingly radical and convergent popular social movement. In concentration camps such as Villa Grimaldi, Tres Álamos, and Puchuncaví, all places where Guillermo Núñez was held captive (Núñez, interview with the author, March 12, 2002), torture was a means to isolate and break down collective activities, induce pain as a fear tactic (one that had reverberations in the wider social sphere), and produce traumatic rupture in its victims. Ultimately, torture fashioned and sealed a culture of silence that lasted even long after its practice was abolished. During the transition to democracy in the 1990s, tens of thousands of torture survivors were all but forgotten by the Chilean state. It became politically more expedient to discuss, however minimally, those who were disappeared or executed than to face the survivors of torture, those who were the nation's living ghosts.

A central tenet of metalevel political violence is that it produces a crisis of national identity, wherein the nation's "system of cultural signification, as the representation of social life" becomes totally destabilized (Bhabha 1990, 2). After crisis, newly rendered nations employ expendable bodies, or what Kelli Lyon-Johnson terms "dead body politics" (2005, 205), as a way to remake national identity, especially through the discourses of nation, social peace, cooperation, and reconciliation. These oft-repeated codes are the human rights rhetoric that later provide grease for the institutions that govern accountability and nation-making. How does art about torture put on view what is concealed by national reconstruction and its institutions that often ossify meaning about the past?

Like other forms of cultural memory (i.e., representations of history with shifting contextual meanings), visual art has the capacity to speak to, contest, elaborate upon, and produce collective experiences that escape the domain of "politics as usual." Núñez's work is a form of cultural memory that makes visible the structural links between bodies in pain and national concealments, thereby providing an alternative narration of nation. Scholars Hornstein and Jacobwitz's edited volume on the Holocaust describes a breadth of cultural forms and spaces of horror (2003). They note the difficult problem of realism and representation but maintain that "the related questions it raises concerning authenticity are not insurmountable" (ibid., 3). Hornstein and Jacobwitz's understanding is that art has the capacity to represent and engage with complex social realities, even though the terrain on which these representations tread is often fraught with difficult ethical questions. They argue that art moves without bounds between history and memory, which makes it suspect in terms of approximating that which cannot be represented (ibid.). Indeed, this very complication of "objective" history versus the constructedness that memory implies has been at the core of my concerns. Visual art carves out new modes of representation that escape the binary logic of history and memory whose reductionist outcome expresses itself as erasure of the experience of violence.

For Núñez, the genre of abstract art offers a means to document the history of state terror while also pursuing the ephemeral, individual, rupturing content of memories. But the nefarious and shifting topic exceeds the canvas of abstraction. Beyond his paintings, Núñez's installation art, interactive media, and testimonial allow him to approach what are indeed the politics and aesthetics of unrepresentable subject matter. Rather than constrain and contain the experiential dimension of torture, Núñez's aesthetic politics recuperates the plenitude of meanings of living with and after torture.

FORMATIONS

Leading up to and during Allende's presidency, national consciousness was in a period of heteroglossia, opening up to multiplicity not just within the economic realm of socialism as "the better alternative" (as a binary view of the period might have it), but also within the arts, music, and theater, producing an expanded view of the possible. Guillermo Núñez is the emblematic figure for a generation of artists, filmmakers, and intellectuals who saw another road for Chile, a path of possibility meant to redress historical injustice and the lack of civil liberties for the nation's excluded populations. They worked toward this goal, however uneven their efforts may have been, however unfulfilled the promise may remain. Of the same generation as the great painter Roberto Matta, Núñez began his career in art during the 1950s. Working first in theater as a costume and set designer, he later turned to painting and installation art, which felt natural to him. While in

Figure 11. Guillermo Núñez, *No hay tiempo para el olvido*, 1963. Oil on canvas.

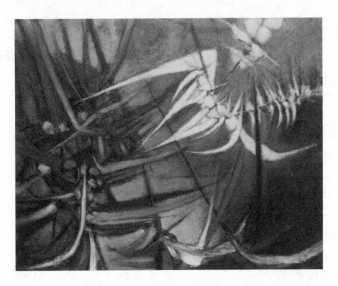

Figure 12. Guillermo Núñez, *No hay tiempo para el olvido*, 1963. Oil on canvas.

theater, he knew my grandfather, a reporter turned theater director who had taken refuge in Chile to escape fascism in Europe. This familial connection with Núñez emerged as we sat talking under the avocado trees by his house (March 29, 2002). The irony of their experiences was not lost on me: in 1975, Núñez was an exile in my grandfather's country of origin, France, seeking refuge from fascist Chile.

Even prior to Núñez's own experience as a survivor of torture, his art reflected a deep concern and engagement with violence and its effects, expressing an explicitly Leftist politics and social agenda. Issues of collective memory and forgetting, central concerns in his paintings of the last thirty years, are eerily anticipated in two abstract paintings of 1963, both titled *No hay tiempo para el olvido* (There Is No Time to Forget) (figs. 11 and 12), a phrase he would use thirty years later to politicize young audiences at the University of Macul while speaking of his own encounter with torture. In these works, there was already a technical effort to imagine and communicate the intimate specter of violence.

Núñez's career has been marked to an extraordinary degree by the history of politics in the nation. The most poignant instance of this was his role as director of the National Museum of Contemporary Art during Allende's term, a highly visible role given the merger of culture and politics during that era. Poetry, literature, murals, music, popular theater, film production, and performance pooled from a rich and diverse set of cultural nationalist and avant-garde movements, flowing into a massive cultural effort that ultimately reflected the ideals, contentions, and ideologies that brought Allende to power in 1970.[6] In the paintings chosen for a 1993 retrospective entitled "Retrato hablado" (Police Sketch) from this earlier period, it is clear that Núñez was in dialog with national and international artistic movements, even while his subject matter addressed political violence and its afterlife around the world. The techniques Núñez developed to communicate violence were later used to denounce Pinochet's military dictatorship, a move consonant with his art of social engagement.[7] By 1974 Núñez's artistic work explicitly criticized the Chilean dictatorship and its violence, a dangerous practice amid the increasing murders, disappearances, and detentions.[8] A major event in Núñez's career was an exhibition he inaugurated in Santiago on March 20, 1975, where he used objects such as cages and packages that were wired shut to evoke military repression (fig. 13). The exhibit was forcibly closed the morning after it opened, and Núñez was arrested and taken to the Tres Álamos concentration camp.

It is ironic, though not surprising given his politics and the turbulent times that Núñez first painted on themes of violence that occurred in other nations and then was directly affected by it in his country of origin. As he states, "I was always concerned with violence in other places. I painted themes related to Vietnam and the war. My work dealt with the violent situation in the U.S. South and violations against African Americans, and with Auschwitz. And all of a sudden violence came here, and those things happened to me" (interview, March 12, 2002).

Núñez's insight that later "those things happened to me" is a useful way to think about the transformation in his position and perspective, namely from informed political subject to torture survivor. In many ways this shift connects his subjectivity and artistic efforts to the broader social movement of survivors of military dictatorships (and U.S. intervention) in the region. During the mid-1970s, when he was exiled to France, it gave his art an important testimonial dimension. In Europe, Núñez's art about

Figure 13. Guillermo Núñez, *¿Y qué hacemos con Leonardo?* 1975.
Mixed media.

terror resonated within the context of the World War II aftermath and within the rising tide of progressive politics, anticolo-
nialism, and anti-intervention sentiments.[9] In stark contradis-
tinction, after returning to Chile in the late eighties Núñez found
himself in a cultural desert, and the press barely noticed his presence (interview, March 12, 2002). This lack of attention was due
in part to the Pinochet regime's discourses and practices of erasure of the Allende period, as well as to the fact that Núñez was
caught within the web of the multiple, often negative, narratives
about returning exiles.[10]

Symbols with abstract national meaning that were recurrent in
Núñez's earlier work were now used as references to his personal
encounters with captivity and exile. Emblematic of this is his 1979

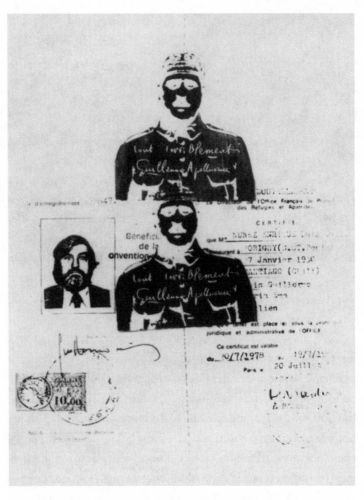

Figure 14. Guillermo Núñez, *Libertad condicional*, 1979. Drawing and serigraph.

work entitled *Libertad condicional* (Parole) (fig. 14), where Núñez superimposes duplicate self-portraits photocopied in negative space onto his national identification card. Across the self-portraits is text in French, which highlights his position as exile, in-between national categories of citizenship. In the juxtaposition between the self-portraits and his identification photo, Núñez finds a trope for exile, a symbol of the rupture between the state's contract with its citizens. With the duplicate images he also expresses the ontology of national exclusion and the search for individual subjectivity beyond the state's authoritative instantiation. In other words, Núñez's national identification was literally and figuratively stripped from him through the violence enacted on his body and subjectivity, calling attention to the inexpressible self-identification outside the constitution of the citizen-subject. Accordingly, the work expresses dislocation, deterritorialization, and emasculation as byproducts of the authoritarian government, itself a byproduct of the exclusions of nation.

In Núñez's effort to reference torture he continues his aesthetic preference for and involvement with abstract art, enabling him to approximate the nefarious and unperceivable character of torture.[11] He explains, "These works are uncompromising. The more you look inside them, the uglier they get" (interview, March 12, 2002). What one also sees is the narration of historical memory. For instance, *Contigo en Tejas Verdes. Contigo en Bucalemu, Colina, Grimaldi, Colliguay, contigo Marta Ugarte, compañero Lucho, compañero Juan* (With you in Tejas Verdes. With you in Bucalemu, Colina, Grimaldi, Colliguay, with you Marta Ugarte, companion Lucho, companion Juan) (1976) displays three bodies severed in parts, strung up, and suspended in the air in distorted positions (fig. 15). Blood, symbolized through strips of paint in various shades of red,

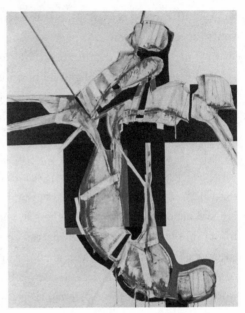

Figure 15.
Guillermo Núñez,
Contigo en Tejas Verdes.
Contigo en Bucalemu,
Colina, Grimaldi,
Colliguay, contigo
Marta Ugarte,
compañero Lucho,
compañero Juan,
1976. Acrylic
on canvas.

travels through the capillaries of the figures, and spills out at a number of points onto a mostly white backdrop. Brown and blue blocks highlight the figures. The bodies, along with the title, stand for the many unnamed in the torture session.

Núñez portrays torture as a fracturing of temporality, where pain is felt through the entire body at once, as symbolized by the screaming mouth and groin (fig. 16). By displaying multiple bodies as small and floating in space, Núñez visualizes how torture produces dissociation of space, while also implying that it literally and metaphorically diminishes the tortured subject's humanity (fig. 17). In such depictions, the painter forces recognition in the viewer of the temporal and spatial dislocations of the torture scene from the perspective of the victim. Again, these images are

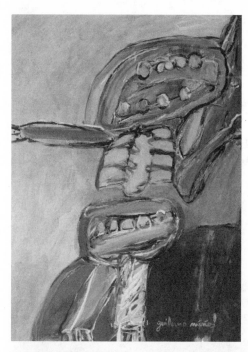

Figure 16. Guillermo
Núñez, *La suite de
Boësses*, 1986. Acrylic
on canvas.

Figure 17. Guillermo
Núñez, *Le déjeuner
sur l'herbe*, 1989.
Acrylic on canvas.

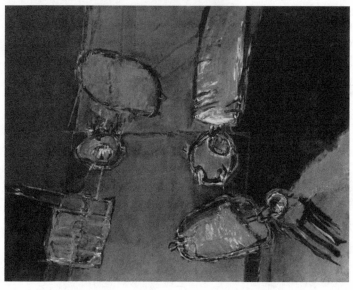

not easily consumable—one reason that Núñez continues to collect thousands of them in a rusted warehouse. "Would you want one of these hanging over your dining room table?" he asked me (interview, March 12, 2002).

Read in their social and political milieu, Núñez's paintings insist on returning to the original torture scene as a way to screen out oblivion, or its opposite, the hypervisibility of torture within public arenas.[12] Expanding further, equating torture with rupture is a focal point for Núñez's art, precisely because it speaks to the wider process of individual and social rupture, and the unfinished and impossible business of psychological resolutions that are imagined in national reconciliation. In this move by power to render and reintegrate national subjects, an increasingly globalized effort to manage the aftermath of large-scale political violence, the tortured subject is diminished by the discursive weight of reconciliation.

TRAUMATIC RUPTURE

So far, I have avoided to some extent the term *trauma*, since its usage is vexed within multiple and often competing discourses, and its concept is historically overdetermined and possibly exhausted. Even so, it is impossible to talk about the repetition of Núñez's torture scenes without invoking a long genealogy of the term *trauma* and the force of violence on the individual psyche. Social trauma is a condition produced by ruptures and violence that frequently arise from large-scale modern events. The term *trauma* is often classified within a decidedly Western clinical conceptualization, oriented at the level of the individual. According to trauma studies, the psyche has mechanisms with which to deal with encounters of rupture. For instance, the act of constriction refers to the process by which painful memories are "split off from ordinary awareness," a frequent reaction of people who have been traumatized (Herman 1997, 45).[13] Sometimes constriction produces amnesia, although with trauma survivors it often functions as a dialectical process, moving between the two extremes of intrusion: the flooding of traumatic memories and their constriction. For Judith Herman, one characteristic expression of trauma is the desire to avoid situations that remind the person of the past, an emotional and psychological mechanism that resists contact with anything reminiscent of the original traumatic event (ibid., 47). Herman's description of trauma is corroborated by psychoanalytic accounts in Chile, where professionals have been working with victims of political violence for the past thirty years.[14] Thus, one way to read the culture of amnesia in Chile is to suggest that while some people transform their suffering into activism, others psychologically move to forget that which simulates the original traumatic encounter.

Of course, there are a number of critiques to the concept of trauma as a diagnostic category. Some consider it a Western artifact, the product of what scholars Rebecca Saunders and Kamran Aghaie call "a specific sociopolitical and clinical genealogy that emerges with late modernity and is assembled out of Euro-American experiences of industrialization and warfare, its gender relations, and its conceptions of normalcy and deviance" (2005, 18). After all, as Saunders and Aghaie thoughtfully observe, it is easier and cheaper to pathologize individuals than to dismantle systems of war, racism, patriarchy, empire, or economic inequality. Increasingly, there is a tendency to think through collective trauma and forms of remembering the past in public and alternative public spheres. My entrance into these matters is more closely aligned with Ann Cvetkovich's compelling work on lesbian public cultures that, as she suggests, desire "to seize authority over trauma discourses from medical and scientific discourse in order to place it back in the hands of those who make culture, as well as forge new models for how affective life can serve as a foundation for public culture" (2003, 20). In these conversations there is a pressing concern with reversing the dissolution of Self that occurs in crisis conditions, where the Self is reintegrated into the social, political, and collective dimension of trauma's original and reiterating production. In Chile, these processes include the incomplete project of incorporation of subaltern subjects during nation-building in the nineteenth century, civil rights struggles that led to state terrorism during the twentieth century, the subsequent reification of a free market, reentrance into the global market, and later the democratic transition. The moment of rupture caused by state terrorism—torture, sexual violence, disappearance, exile—cannot be separated from the subsequent work of its individual and collective integration into the practice of everyday life. Núñez's art provides a model for public democratic culture as a visualization of torture's ongoing integration.

EXPENDABLE BODIES AND TORTURE'S SCREEN

Within the fractures of violence, nation states depend on the framework of democracy and truth commissions as formats for producing a new national identity. The "expendable bodies" of political violence are not merely surplus, or of limited value, but central figures of political staging that work to rebrand the nation in violence's aftermath.[15] Thus, one of the central locations of globalization—indeed, where it gains traction at the level of the nation state—is in the rhetoric and framework of establishing political democracy, which for nations in transition means human rights investigations, commissions, and reports. As Saskia Sassen suggests, "important components of globalization" are in fact "embedded in particular institutional locations within national territories" (1998, xxix). For Chile, the institutionalization of victims' stories initially occurred by describing the most horrendous and extreme cases of human rights violations and those that resulted in physical death, first through the Rettig Report (1991) and later through the National Roundtable for Dialog (1998).[16] Only in 2004, under Ricardo Lagos's administration, were cases of torture considered worthy of full-scale investigation, namely through the National Commission on Political Imprisonment and Torture Report, commonly known as the Valech Report. These institutional moments of human rights discourse have rewritten the past with the state's presentist objectives in mind, namely to continue economic liberalization and install political democracy. Until very recently (most notably on September 6, 2006, when former dictator Pinochet was stripped of immunity), accountability through the legal realm had been severely curtailed. Prior to 2002, institutional barriers (e.g., the 1978 Amnesty Law, the 1980 Constitution, and a corrupt tribunal court system) had made it all but impossible for the crimes of the dictatorship to be legally prosecuted, even while human rights rhetoric and reports continued to signal that the excesses of the past had been squarely addressed.

As was true in many Latin American authoritarian regimes, torture was a main strategy of counterinsurgency, a highly organized activity, and a public secret, illustrated by the (then meaningful) fact the Pinochet dictatorship insisted on a series of qualifications and exceptions to the rules before signing the United Nations Convention against Torture (see Comisión Nacional contra la Tortura 1989). As former President Lagos acknowledges, about 94 percent of more than thirty thousand documented detainees who were detailed in the Valech Report experienced the rupture of torture and 95 percent of female torture victims experienced sexual torture (2004). Specialized techniques were gleaned and imported from the United States and Brazil, including methods known as the submarine *(submarino)*, the grill *(parrilla)* (see fig. 5), and the parrot's perch *(pau de arara)*, or being hung from a rod by the wrists. Physical torture was accompanied by psychological methods, such as forcing victims to view another's torture. Torturers threatened captives with physical and emotional pain not only as a means to retrieve information but also as a way to instill fear and resignation in victims and a culture of fear in the nation (Weinstein and Lira 1987, 33). Incorporated into all detentions, torture was used against tens of thousands of Allende supporters, MIR activists, members of the Christian Left and socialist and communist parties, and anyone that allegedly supported or, for that matter, was deemed in some way to be close to one of these affiliations (Asociación de Abogados 1980, 7).

Although some human rights organizations and efforts exerted political pressure, the military regime continued to deny the existence of torture, even until the end of the dictatorship and beyond. As government spokesperson Orlando Poblete said, "In Chile, nobody is tortured. There is no repression and our government is founded on respect for the rights of individuals" (Amnesty International Report 1987). One would imagine that the revelation of systematic torture would be integral to the project of democracy from 1990 forward. Instead, the ubiquitous torture on detainees and the pervasive sexual torture of female bodies went unmentioned in the 1991 Rettig Report, which instead focused on political executions and disappearances.[17] Moreover, the political and social justice effects of the report were further contained through a series of high-level negotiations, including the Peace Proposal, the legislation that upheld the 1978 Amnesty Law that exempted military officials and agents of the state from legal prosecution for murder and torture.[18] Highlighting select cases of torture, disappearance, and death rather than exposing the massiveness and persistence of the torture problem was the strategy of the transition government, composed of "successfully integrated" returned exiles, to foster social peace.

The pact of transition had to evolve to respond to unfolding global events, such as Pinochet's London arrest and attempted extradition to Spain. The 2004 Valech Report, detailing the cases of some thirty thousand survivors, emerged from the political terrain opened by Pinochet's attempted extradition and again effectively rewrote the past, this time reworking the state's own silence about the pervasiveness of torture. In broad terms, the report provided survivors with overdue symbolic compensation (in the form of recognition) and laid the foundation for material compensation (in the form of pensions); it also helped pave the way for Michelle Bachelet's 2006 presidential victory, as she herself was a survivor of torture.[19]

One of the untenable differences with respect to torture is precisely between official discourse and its demand for narrative disclosure and the experiential prediscursive moment of torture's rift. Tellingly, the state, through the Valech Report, imagines that it can reincorporate torture survivors into the nation state by awarding material pensions and printing testimonials (regardless of how anonymously these stories show up in national reports). In stark contrast, Guillermo Núñez continues to narrate torture as a space of exclusion from the nation state. In this way, his repetitive symbols of the body in pain are consonant with his reflections about the contemporary political scene.

On one level, Núñez's paintings of these repetitions might be interpreted as a creative reenactment of the psychic disintegration that torture produces, a process that holds an individual therapeutic utility for the artist. At times, Núñez himself even suggests as much: "It doesn't matter to me what others think. This is what I want to be released from me" (interview, March 12, 2002). Yet considering the political agency Núñez has always expressed, the repetitive motifs take on a different meaning. As Raquel Olea comments, "The political sign of Núñez's work remembers things forgotten, observes the naked reality within white nothingness" (1993, 65). The white nothingness that Olea mentions and that Núñez's paintings make visible is the absence of social justice through redress for those who continue to bear the consequences of state terror in their bodies, and in their daily lives.

Saidiya Hartman has commented eloquently on the link between redress and social justice, and her discussion is useful for understanding political democracy's inability to approximate redress in the aftermath of torture. In the case of slavery, as she argues, redress means and meant the restitching of the social fabric, or what she terms the "re-membering of the social body" (1997, 76). However, conditions of captivity and enslavement are violent forms of rupture that usher an enormous breach, making it impossible to "re-member." Hartman poignantly states that "efforts to set things right would entail a revolution of the social order—the abolition of slavery, racism, domination and exploitation, the realization of justice and equality and the fulfillment of needs" (ibid.).

When measured against Hartman's description, the attempts of political systems of democracy, especially in the earlier period of transition in Chile, fall short. Núñez's paintings, his personal and artistic trajectory, and his testimonial of the practice of torture illustrate the incompleteness of the current project of political democracy to set things right after torture. The rift between the state and torture survivors is precisely the break between political democracy and its demand for narrative disclosure on the one hand, and the experiential legacy of torture that is inevitably ongoing and exceeds the boundaries of linear temporal mandates on the other. Guillermo Núñez's art exposes the impossibility of redressing torture through institutional channels like state efforts at reconciliation. In fact, his art and testimony suggests that the only way to redress torture is to make social justice a living, breathing practice.

BEHIND THE BLINDFOLD

The politics of Núñez's art on torture, like its counterpart in literary works and performance art during the dictatorship,[20] puts emphasis on the body as a site of violence, displacement, witness, and contestation. Núñez uses abstract and installation arts as means to represent the nefarious and unperceivable character of torture.[21] Perhaps the most recognizable and often repeated motif of Núñez's art is the blindfold. In April 2002, I attended his exhibit "¿Qué hay en el fondo de tus ojos?" (What is there in the depth of your eyes?). What lies behind (or remains after) torture was the central meaning of the blindfold metonym. The walls in one of the rooms of the exhibit were covered with sketches of ex-prisoners' faces. Núñez had made large negative-space sketches from photographs that were published in the newspaper, pictures that were taken before the people were captured. He transformed these photos into two-foot-square black-and-white images. Núñez had painted in four of the sketches, two of which had the eyes covered by blindfolds and were sketched in a torment of bold colors and dripping paint (fig. 18). Next to his completed sketches, Núñez hung unfinished copies of the same faces, to be later filled in by spectators. He invited participants to visually conjure their own captivity by drawing their own rendering of the world lived behind the blindfold. In this way, Núñez imagined a shift in perspective from observer to painting what is behind the eyes or what lies within, a shift to interiority rather than the surface effects of scars, bruises, and deformation, quintessential evidentiary markers of torture sessions. In this work Núñez asks for a pure moment of empathy, where the witness perspective collapses into that of the tortured Other. Is it possible or politically desirable to approximate torture through the imagination without direct experience of its pain? Does this approximation by the spectator become transformed in a way that ultimately diminishes the alterity and rupture of torture's experience?

On the exhibit floor, at the entrance to the room with the faces, Núñez painted illegible words, as if to emphasize language's inability to express the experience of torture. In one corner of the exhibit's entrance was a large table with scissors, pens, and pastel crayons, and a note that beckoned people to trace their own hand, cut out the drawing, and hang it on the wall. Indeed, several dozen tracings were already pinned up and imprinted with each person's signature. The makeshift hand memorial resembled both the

Figure 18. Guillermo Núñez, *¿Qué hay en el fondo de tus ojos?* 2002. Pen on paper.

posters of the relatives of the disappeared asking *¿Dónde están?* (Where are they?) and memorials such as those described in the previous chapter. On the same table, Núñez had left a mirror inviting spectators to look at themselves, while asking them to also think about the exhibit's central question, "What lies at the depth of your eyes?" This prompt offered exhibit participants the possibility of an interior retreat, while gesturing toward the issue of subject recognition as a means to contrast the fractures of identity that torture produces in its subject. Núñez forced attention to the body (through the face and hands), to subjectivity (through the mirror), to torture (through the blindfold and illegible words), and to disappearance and death (through the makeshift wall of hands). Ultimately, Núñez produced an exhibit that, through a series of familiar icons, forced self-witnessing and public memory of state terror and its effects.

Through his speeches and images Núñez asks audiences and spectators to produce for themselves the space of terror and torture by locating themselves behind the blindfold and thus within the experience of the prisoner. While on the one hand Núñez may want too pure a space of empathy, he also offers the experience of torture as a ritual of social connection. Diana Taylor conceives of "memories and survival strategies [as] transmitted from one generation to another through performative practices that include (among other things) ritual, bodily and linguistic practices" (2003, 108). Núñez's work is a ritual process of transgenerational communication. His testimonial of his blindfolded captivity is also an important performance of gender vulnerability. By discussing the blockage to his sight by power through the symbol of the blindfold, Núñez unhinges the idea of the stoic masculine. In this way, he shows the male body as a site of power's inscription and revolutionary defeat.[22] Thus, his interactive art practice is a form of dissemination of what was lived through the body during and after collective terror.

Addressing his own blindfolded imprisonment is another important aspect of Núñez's performative work about the tortured body (pers. comm., March 29, 2002). At the closing event, a male student from the audience commented, "You paint and express the victim and the perpetrator. What force is there in the border between what is seen and what is not seen?" Núñez replied, "In 1974 I had my eyes blindfolded day and night. I realized that I began to retreat into the world of imagination behind the eyes. No one has painted this world from where the spectator can imagine the situation." Thus, the retreat into interiority becomes the condition and response to torture, and painting constructs a bridge to exteriority.

As Elaine Scarry has noted, the idea that pain is inherently inexpressible and unshareable is made acute in cases of torture, where speaking is shut down (1985). In many ways the incommunicability of the experience of torture is not from the inability to narrate the experience, as the recent testimonials from Abu Ghraib have shown, but the inability to represent the complexity and fullness of that which escapes narrative description. This produces an irony, since the dialectic of silence and narration is a core aspect of torture. The experience begs to be known among both those who have lived through it and those who were in its proximity, including survivors, perpetrators, and those whose feigned ignorance amounted to complicity.

Núñez's project, in fact, is to communicate the unimaginable to the spectator by shining a spotlight on the scene of torture. By repeating the symbol of the blindfold he makes visible the ongoing confrontation of the body and psyche with torture, the process of remembering that the blindfold unleashes, the retreat to imagination that the blindfold forces, and the blindness of the nation to the deep breach that systematic torture produced. From power's perspective, the blindfold is a means to disorient and produce fear, taking away the ability to mediate the social world. In turn, the prisoner retreats inward into imagination and unto the self, not only as a form of escape or dissociation from reality but as a form of survival.

For Núñez, the very sight that was stripped by power becomes the source of narrating experience, namely through his paintings. If, as Elaine Scarry suggests, language fails in its apprehension of the body in pain because of the rupture of Self that torture produces (1985, 3–59), then the painted image may be a better repository than verbal testimonial or narration for communicating experience and sentience. After torture, when Núñez's vision was returned, the blindfold became a way to attenuate, for the viewer, the unavailable location of difference that it produced.

Núñez's art is also a source of evidence of what happened in the concentration camps of Chile, particularly under conditions where little, if any, visual documentation exists. Not much photographic evidence is available on collective violence during a dictatorship. Of course, film, tape recorders, and other modern forms of documentation rarely capture secret atrocities. This is where drawings, sketches, and descriptions of compounds by survivors fill in absence, the blind spots outside the photograph. Although I do not assume a transparent relationship between evidence and accountability, part of the invisibility of Latin American authoritarian violence, like that of the colonial violence before it, stems from the lack of photographic documentation of atrocity. Unlike the Nazi concentration camps during World War II,[23] Chile's camps have produced few photographs of atrocities, making Núñez's art an archive of the period and of torture's persistent effects. Cultural representation and visual testimonial thus become invaluable evidence of the state's dirty work during the 1970s, helping to trace its itinerary and convey its experience.

As María Angélica Illanes suggests, not only is Núñez's artwork an important repository of memory, but it also does important cultural work in the battle over remembering and documenting the past (2002, 13). His art is a form of cultural memory that unearths what is missed by the project of national reconstruction and institutional processes of accountability. In this way, culture offers another means to remember and reimagine the nation after crisis (Walkowitz and Knauer 2004).

IF THE PERIOD leading up to the military dictatorship was characterized by a wider acceptance of the nation's multiplicity, then the tortured body represents the truncation of the possible (the severing of heteroglossia), where silence is what remains. Through abstraction and installation, visual art offers another method of making this history public. Since the social body is in need of repair after trauma, by re-membering the history of brutality, ruptured social relations, and the body in pain, Núñez opens the possibility for a democratic future. Unlike the state efforts of reconciliation and limited accountability, which bring a limited form of democracy, cultural production about torture returns to the moment of rupture as a means to wrestle with the present's past. Guillermo Núñez's artistic practice of memory, reenactment, and narration performs cultural work about the body in pain that gives visual language to experiences that a tortured subjectivity is unable to move on from, to reconcile, or to forget. One of the material objectives of this memory aesthetic is to excavate the nation's investments in neoliberal progress within public spheres such as universities and poor communities, where Núñez often displays and gives away his art. Núñez's art contests the logic of consumer culture because his paintings do not easily circulate within art markets. For all they contribute to historical understanding of the systematic use of torture in the nation and its later occlusion, they are not visually easy to digest.

As Núñez ironically asks, "Why does it matter what that old man paints?" (pers. comm., March 29, 2002). The perspective of the tortured subject can be confusing within a hegemonic discursive regime that is keen to publicize economic success, while downplaying (at least until the Valech Report) the bodies that display these consequences. Núñez speaks to a past that recalls the defeat of socialism in a present when neoliberalism is unchallenged. In a rare public admission of this coupling, one official declared, "We should ask for forgiveness for not having believed in private property and the market."[24] Núñez's art frames the stabilizing logic of such couplings by recognizing how the remnants of torture in the public sphere—the shadow spaces that political democracy only tentatively touches—can construct openings toward a true democratic culture.

4

Documenting Absence

Ghostly Screens Unsettle the Past

One year prior to Pinochet's house arrest in London for an extradition to Spain that never happened, Patricio Guzmán made the now classic documentary *Chile, Obstinate Memory* (1997), a powerful film that chronicles the director's return trip from exile with his monumental three-part documentary *The Battle of Chile* (1979) in his luggage to screen to audiences that had not been able to view it during the Pinochet regime.[1] The latter film engendered my obsession with the figure of muteness and how it is visually conjured. The documentary's premise is that the memory of authoritarian violence was concealed and obscured in the nation's public spheres, a silence that the director confronts with his own documentation of the Allende revolution and its very public demise over the later months of 1972 and throughout 1973. Hoping to counter memory's obstinate character during political democracy, Guzmán returned from France to screen *The Battle of Chile* to select Chilean audiences, including schoolchildren, students at public and private universities, and former Allende bodyguards. *Obstinate Memory*

records their reactions to that earlier film, which had not had significant circulation within the country, even though it had won international acclaim.[2] The film's dramatic ending captures a group
of about fifteen Left-leaning university students as they watch the
closing scene of *The Battle of Chile*, where the military is busy raid-
ing poor neighborhoods and severely repressing its residents; afterward several students are visibly shaken, although one is asleep
(a testament to the film's monumental length). In this stirring scene,
students struggle through words and gestures to convey what they
were too young to understand at the time, sharing their sense of
shame and feelings of despair. Most poignant is the painful reaction and tormented face of a young man who, after watching the
military's brutality and reading Allende's final speech, is reduced
to a flood of tears and barely audible whimpers. His muted image
expresses and condenses the national public silence about the costs
and signification of collective violence, and the persistence of the
enactment of social rupture and pain on subsequent generations.[3]
Muteness is not always devoid of political potentiality, conventional wisdom notwithstanding, especially when it expresses itself
on documentary screens.

Another cinematic figure of muteness appears in Silvio Caiozzi's
Fernando ha vuelto (Fernando Returns) (1998), released, ironically,
the same year of Pinochet's arrest. In a strikingly concise and
densely codified documentary, Fernando Olivares Mori's body returns after a twenty-five-year absence. As his mother expresses
with great difficulty, "He returns, but not alive." Her image is disturbing, as I discuss later in this chapter, and asks for contemplation about the notion of the "resilient human spirit," a liberal narration about how violence can always be worked out. Fernando's
mother has not yet recovered from the event of state violence,

suffering the disappearance of her son with such acuteness as to be rendered almost mute. As these cinematic moments illustrate and as I elaborate in the following pages, documentary film shows the panoply of social subjects that continue to live with violence, long after its initial rupture. It also makes visible the sites of memory's exclusion within public spheres of the postdictatorship.

Although the multiple layers of mediation that are present in the documentary may lay suspicion for what a film whose focus is another film, such as *Obstinate Memory*, can say about "observable reality," a more flexible path to knowledge invites us to see how film subjects and film audiences can have an evocative and meaningful social relationship to these productions. Jeffrey R. Middents rightly points out that the subjects of *Obstinate Memory* "are also spectators, much like us, who are currently watching a documentary. As such, they function in a sort of associative fashion with us as fellow spectators" (2005, 188). More broadly, in the genre of documentary, as Bill Nichols argued some time ago, audiences expect "sounds and images [to] bear an indexical relation to the historical world" (1991, 27).

The expectation of a match between events and reality in a location like postauthoritarian Chile is heightened, because of the political character of the documentary genre's history in the nation and throughout Latin America, where the commitment to social issues follows a long aesthetic trajectory.[4] The form of politics documented in these films is an affective and bodily encounter with memory, which Jane M. Gaines names as a political mimesis that is "about a relationship between bodies in two locations— on the screen and in the audience—and it is the starting point for the consideration of what the one body makes the other do" (1999, 90).[5] Gaines contends that films serve a distinct political purpose that sensually appeals to audiences, whereby the "aesthetic of similarity" bridges the ontology of the screen and that of the audience (ibid.). The aesthetic of similarity is an illusion that is based on documentary film's evidentiary status. In the case of Chile, documentary becomes a visual and sound archive of memories; when such documentaries get publicly screened, they can create spaces where forms of public memory about political violence can be meaningfully experienced. Furthermore, embedded within the narratives of these films and understood by the audiences that screen them are many moments of intersubjective identification, where documentary offers the opportunity for socially breaking through and witnessing the hegemony of public silence, concealment, or the flattening of the complex subjectivities of loss and survival. These moments, I contend, travel beyond the mass-media sound bites about the dictatorship past as forms of knowing "the Other"—those directly and indirectly affected by loss, trauma, censorship, and other structured forms of repressing history, including the absence of the body through disappearance. In the end, the social sphere is an important and necessary place to conjure, discuss, work through, and unsettle memories of collective violent events that originate from state terror, and the addition of documentary film performs a social narrative function ("Entrevista a Silvio Caiozzi" 1999, 16). Although it may appear as if the original experience of disappearance is profoundly personal and familial, painful effects are collectively registered and in need of social expression (ibid.).

In the aftermath of state violence, the social costs were not evenly distributed among female and male subjects. Caiozzi's and Guzmán's documentaries emphasize the familiar narrative that males were the main targets of military repression and that mothers, daughters, and sisters bore the greatest emotional burden of violence's effects. The problem with this rendition is that the female subjects in the films are reified as sufferers and victims of the nation, and female revolutionary subjectivity is cast as marginal. In contrast, Marilú Mallet's film *La cueca sola* (They Danced Alone) (2003), which I discuss toward the end of the chapter, creates a feminist genealogy of social struggle and experience, which nuances the effects of collective violence and locates female agency within a broader spectrum of the identities mediated by, and emerging out of, authoritarianism.

SCENES OF WITNESS

The effects of losing a family member are perhaps worse under conditions of disappearance, when there is no physical body to mourn. Those disappeared are "absent" objects, both invoking fear in the populous and posing as an obstacle to mourning for family members (Robben 2000, 87).[6] As Robben has argued, there is an emotional and psychological need for material burial, since communal ritual with loved ones materializes the passage from life to physical death (ibid.). Silvio Caiozzi's documentary *Fernando ha vuelto* films the dramatic identification by Chilean forensic scientists of Fernando Olivares Mori's skeleton, a corpse that finally returns home.

Fernando was an MIR activist during the Allende years who in 1973 was disappeared by the Pinochet regime; only much later were his bones exhumed from Patio 29, the infamous collective burial site in the Santiago General Cemetery, which continues to be a site of unmarked tombs (fig. 19). Although his bones were found in 1991, his remains were not identified until 1998 by the

Figure 19. The infamous Patio 29 at the Santiago General Cemetery, June 25, 2002. Photo by Nicole Hayward.

Servicio Médico Legal (Legal Medical Service), a process to which Caiozzi's camera bears witness by filming the display of Fernando's skeleton and Agave Díaz's "reencounter" with her husband. In the film, we meet Fernando's family, including his widow, son, and very ill mother, and follow them on their painful journey through the identification and ultimate burial of his bones. The spectator is asked to witness the reality of dictatorship violence, its horrors and its excess, by watching a victim's family recover only recently identified remains. The film's low budget quality and charged affective tone, rendered through testimonials by family members in direct address, give a sense of immediacy and urgency to the film's subject. Indeed, Caiozzi told me how he literally stumbled upon the subject of the documentary: he had brought a camera with him to the identification appointment, which he attended because he was a very close family friend of Fernando's widow. The story of the film's origin again references documentary's assumed indexicality and its privileged claim of authenticity (interview with the author, April 11, 2002).[7]

The film premiered at the Valdivia International Film Festival in October 1998 and won first prize. It provided a form of cathartic witness for audiences, for those drawn to viewing such a film would have also been affected to varying degrees by state terrorism. As Caiozzi told me, this was the first time he experienced such a powerful reaction to the screening of any of his works. He recounted how, during the question-and-answer period he hosted after the screening, audience members were quiet at first and then one by one stood up in the theater to give their own testimonies, much to his astonishment. As the audience was leaving, several people who were visibly moved approached the filmmaker, describing their own encounter with state violence. In this way, the film helped release indescribable pain for those who had witnessed and suffered during the dictatorship. At later screenings as well, audience members would cry during the film and the question-and-answer periods; afterward, they too approached Caiozzi with their experiences of violence, torture, and death, and their survival through the process of incomplete justice, acknowledgment, and unending grief (interview with the author, May 15, 2002).

When I spoke to Caiozzi, he discussed how the film circulated very minimally in Chile, although it had won several prizes in Europe, as well as in Havana, Cuba. Since its debut in Valdivia, it has been shown only in smaller venues and at odd hours on Sky cable television. It was not altogether censored, he suggested, but there seemed to be little interest in showing "this kind of material" in the most public venues of the nation. When Silvio Caiozzi mentioned his dismay at its circulation, I had to remind him that the film was released just before Pinochet's November 1998 arrest, at a time when victims of crimes had no recourse to justice and acts of terror were nationally still invisible and unaccepted (ibid.).[8] As such, the issues at the core of the film seem to touch upon conflicted conceptions of the past that producers and media decision makers would rather not confront, either for fear of political or commercial retribution—since there was both continuity and overlap between those who controlled the media and those who supported the dictatorship—or for lack of political will in terms of media programming. What this film and its limited circulation reveal is how in the public realm, and not within the private family (as convention would have it), memories about disappearances and other atrocities continued to be repressed and elided, their persistence underestimated.

FILMIC JOURNEY

The four parts of the film, "The Identification," "The Wait," "The Return," and "The Goodbye," map the four stages of what occurs *after* a disappearance and, for the more fortunate families, toward the recovery of remains. In the film's structure, these parts mark the journey of Fernando's corpse out of the ontological landscape of disappearance into the family's acceptance of the identification and ultimately through the ritual of burial, material markers that are mirrored by a series of painful affective moments and narrative bridges in the film.

The most dramatic scene is Agave Díaz's encounter with the bones of her dead husband.[9] The display of bones on the table is stirring. It recalls representations of a Christ-like ultimate sacrifice, with echoes of the documentary images of Che Guevara's martyrdom, though all that remains of Fernando's body is bones. Agave approaches the table timidly at first, but as the forensic scientists begin to describe the long list of torture and beatings that the body endured, including fifty-five fractures, she moves closer to the bones centered in the camera's view. In a surreal filmic moment, Agave touches the cranium, even resting both hands on what is presumably Fernando's skull.

The first time I viewed this documentary, while cataloging the video archives of the University of Chile's Gender and Culture program, I was astonished and horrified by the image, thinking that Caiozzi had gone beyond the boundaries of public spectacle and drama by choosing not to edit out the scene. In talking with Caiozzi, I asked him about its staging and whether he ever doubted his choice to include it. Here is his reply:

> During postproduction, I began to fear a bit that the viewer would object to not only what one sees as remains, but also how the widow touches and strokes the bones. Later, I made an appointment with Agave at my office to record the testimony of what she was thinking at the moment, to possibly put her voice over the image so that in some respects we could understand her touch. What happened in that moment when the normal reaction might have been a kind of distancing, or I don't know what else? Her response to me was that she felt the bones were warm. "They're warm," she said. "On first seeing them I felt a great impact, but right after that I felt I had to take the bones, that I had to touch them, and that the bones were warm, but I also had to give them warmth." (Agave Díaz quoted by Silvio Caiozzi)

For Caiozzi, Agave's urge to pick up and touch her husband's "warm" bones is a gesture of familiarity and closeness, rather than the distancing and abjection of his remains that characterized the military's stance about those captured. Agave's gesture brings Fernando back into the space of the living, resemanticizing the remains as cherished. The bones felt warm to her because she had the chance to encounter the materiality of her husband's remains and in return offer comfort to them. In fact, her affective and spontaneous response crystallized for me the experience of a living, rather than finalized, death among family members of the disappeared. That Agave feels close to her husband's bones after twenty-five years of material separation makes an important point about the experience of time for relatives of victims, namely bringing into relief the contradictions between this time-sense and institutional notions of forgetting based upon linear time, with its correlative statement "time will heal all wounds." Agave's reaction in the scene, instead, unearths how the personal space of affect is immune from such modernist and teleological constructions of time and healing. But the singular image of the couple's haunting reunion also draws attention to the unbounded sense of loss in the ontology of disappearance, where physical remains or narratives of finality are inexistent. Furthermore, Agave inverts the stereotype of the passive, grieving widow by showing a deep reservoir of strength and insight when she, in essence, touches death and makes the skeleton part of the family's ritual of mourning. As such, her act challenges the viewer to accept the conversation between death and the living that the gesture intimates. By leaving this scene in, Caiozzi offers space for Agave to visualize a different conception of death, with more porous boundaries between the dead and the living, than the Western imagining of death as separation and finality.

Like this moment, there are several other images of grief, remains, identification, and martyrdom in the film that work at the limits of visual comprehension. Indeed, the success of *Fernando ha vuelto* in staging the effects of disappearance is its ability to affectively position viewers, mostly through the camera's intimate view, to understand the magnitude of our incomprehension. With a shocking effect, another scene emphasizes how difficult it is grasp the concept of disappearance. From the Servicio Médico Legal, Patricia Hernández, a forensic medical doctor, and Isabel Rebeco, a forensic anthropologist, show Agave photos of Fernando's face and bone structure while he was alive, superimposing these images on photos of his skeleton as it was found in Patio 29. Viewing the montage of Fernando as a living being over his skeleton forces the viewer to reckon with the apparently narrow space between life and death. The audio track provides the narrative for the unassimilable image: according to the forensic experts, the wide bone structure of the jaw and especially the large uneven rows of teeth provide irrefutable proof of a positive identification. (In fact, this identification was later called into question and the body reexhumed in 2005, leading Caiozzi to include a coda in his new edition of the documentary, which is titled "Has Fernando Disappeared Again?")[10] They also discuss how the process of identification often takes years, with some family members dying without complete knowledge of whether their disappeared relative was ever correctly identified.

As viewers we identify with the political and humanitarian work of the forensic scientists, rendered through the close-ups on the women's faces as they talk about their work and as one of them smokes cigarettes, an act that renders familiarity. After describing the scientific aspects of the process, Isabel Rebeco turns to the social and personal burdens of the work: "From the beginning it was always difficult. It came with a heavy emotional load, very emotional. First, because we asked ourselves if we were doing it well. Second, because we felt the burden of what it would mean if we were wrong. It's impossible to not get involved. It affects you in your personal life, in your family life; it's stressful; it's saddening. I remember that during the excavation of Patio 29, which lasted fourteen days, I lost twenty pounds. And it was purely out of tension. It's clear that it affects you." Drawing attention to the body as a site of traumatic contagion, the forensic scientist in the film underscores how unearthing and identifying remains has consequences on the health of these workers.

In this scene, the language of science that has been used throughout the film turns personal and reflective as we hear about the emotional, social, and psychological burden on the forensic workers to identify individuals out of often scarce or incomplete remains. Rebeco's wasting body as a result of this work could be interpreted as a physical and metaphorical response to the wasted lives produced by the dictatorship.

REMAINS OF NATION

In a central scene in the film, the link between masculinity, violence, and the role of the military is made explicit. Still in the Servicio Médico Legal, family relatives gather together around Fernando's bones, tightly holding each other's hands as they pray and offer flowers to the dead. Fernando's sister-in-law speaks up, while crying, asking for forgiveness for what the military has done. As a daughter of a military official, she carries the moral burden in the film, saying how she feels utter embarrassment at the military's acts of cruelty. It is telling that a military daughter asks for

symbolic forgiveness for the death work of her father's generation. Like the forensic scientists, who internalize the affective
weight of state violence's shadows, the daughter resituates the
masculinized military acts of murder and denial. These scenes of
apology and demonstrated evidence that the death resulted from
state violence are important in disclosing the extent to which masculinity and violence are bound up and work through the military dictatorship, with gendered outcomes.

Perhaps the pivotal sequence of the film with respect to the
gendered effects of the dictatorship on identity is during "The
Wait,"[11] when we are introduced to Mauricio, Fernando's son,
who grew up with the *presence* of his father's disappearance, which
has shaped his identity over his life as the son of a disappeared. In
a poignant scene of direct address, Mauricio asks, even demands,
that Caiozzi search out the profound pain that Fernando's disappearance has caused, pointing us to Fernando's mother and her
illness. It is night and, as Mauricio holds a candle and walks in
silence with his family members to remember his father, the camera captures his angry and tormented face, expressing the loss of
his father.

In this moment, Mauricio, like Fernando at the offices of the
Servicio Médico Legal, embodies the nation's loss of a revolutionary version of masculinity. Here, Mauricio's loss works as an
inversion of the common conception of "woman as sufferer for
the nation." If the project of dictatorship is to reinstall patriarchy,
it does so through emotionally and physically decimating tens of
thousands of working- and middle-class revolutionary men and
their male offspring, using torture, death, disappearance and
suffering as its instruments.[12]

Mauricio's anger can be seen as an intertextual reference to

Patricio Guzmán's film *Obstinate Memory* (1997), the ending of which records how fifteen young people respond to *The Battle of Chile* (1979) and how the film affects their impressions of the dictatorship. One man, in particular, shows loss through rage, though tears readily run down his face. His outrage and pain at growing up without his brother, who was killed by the military, is expressed through his forceful gestures, a powerful visual moment that registers the pain of younger generations and, in particular, of young men. As he points to his chest, he says, "The pain is still within me; it continues there." Like Mauricio, this young man has come of age within the everyday structures of knowledge and feeling that dictatorship violence and its consequences have imposed. In *Fernando ha vuelto* Mauricio is coded as politically militant; he wears red, which symbolizes either communist or socialist sympathies, his tone implies impatience and anger with slow transitional justice, and at the funeral procession at the film's end he stands in front holding a red banner imprinted with his father's face. For sons and daughters of those who perished, anger, protest, and pain are expressions of social struggle, symbolized by Mauricio's brief appearance in Caiozzi's film.

It is fitting that in *Fernando ha vuelto*, Mauricio introduces us to his grandmother as a visible bearer of the grief of dictatorship at the other end of the generational spectrum. Her testimony is characterized by barely understandable sounds of torment. Apparently, her illness has affected her speech to such an extent that normative tonalities are impossible for her to produce. A caretaker carefully translates the mother's words for the camera. One wonders how the nurse can even make sense of the convoluted sounds, whimpers, and cries that she projects. Mauricio indicates that her illness is the direct result of her son's disappearance, and even twenty-five years later she cannot resolve the fact of his death. "He was twenty-seven years old when he disappeared," she says. "My son returns, but not alive." The emotionally packed scene visually displays the incomprehensible pain the mother has endured; the lives that have been taken from her (both her son's life and her own) are apparent in her inability to modulate. In some ways, the tormented face and words of the mother are more powerful than the translated, smoothed-out testimony by the nurse. The the mother's muteness gestures toward the inexplicability of state violence.

Through another family member's testimonial, the viewer is told that Fernando's mother has birthed six children, whom we see in portraits that hang on the walls of the house. This knowledge only emphasizes her loss, since she is not consoled by the fact that there are five others: as she has said to her family members, she brought six into the world and one was taken from her. The viewer is asked to reckon with the emotional and psychological burden of a mother's loss and her pain that cannot be healed. Again this is a moment where survivors and their relatives' affective experience directly contradicts national efforts to move toward closure. In this sense, the figure of mother as mute and unhealed symbolically denounces both the legacies of state violence and, in parallel fashion, the transition's reconstruction project that casts as marginal those directly affected. Furthermore, Fernando's mother and her lack of narrative clarity interestingly calls forward the Madres de la Plaza de Mayo (Mothers of the Plaza de Mayo, in Buenos Aires), who have so much narrative power. Their celebrated history of female activism, eloquence, and public interventions during authoritarian regimes[13] can be projected against this scene, where the symbolic weight of maternal victimhood is carried by Fernando's mother's disfigured speech and mournful wails.

MOTHERS, FAMILIES, AND NATION

Feminist scholars have shown us how gender regimes of subjection are closely linked to national constructions and constitutions of citizen subjects (Fregoso 2001a; Alarcón, Kaplan, and Moallem 1999). One task has been to challenge what appears to be a normalized construction of nation as a gender-neutral project. Chatterjee leverages an important revision of Benedict Anderson's concept of the Imagined Community, which does not distinguish between power differentials among individuals and groups within nations (1991). To this end, Chatterjee asks a primordial question: Whose imagined community? In a feminist vein, Elspeth Probyn reformulates the question by asking: Whose gender? (1999). As this scholarship shows, the normative heterosexual family, often mobilized for conservative politics, is an institutional site for nation-building projects, extended through the biopolitical state and the ideology of national belonging.[14] Giorgio Agamben reminds us that "modern totalitarianism can be defined as the establishment, by means of the state of exception, of a legal civil war that allows for the physical elimination not only of political adversaries but of entire categories of citizens who for some reason cannot be integrated into the political system" (2005, 2). Of course, female subjects, like poor, indigenous, queer, and "subversive" subjects, are deemed abject by the military state. Even during the constitution of the nation, these subjects were constructed as marginal.

The military state's effort to retraditionalize women in Chile was integral to the counterrevolutionary project and happened in a number of ways. First, the state disarticulated social movements where women were becoming increasingly involved and emerging as visible leaders (including neighborhood soup kitchens, community associations, milk cooperatives, unions, cultural arts movements, the MIR, and the Christian Left) and as Machi (healers) in Mapuche communities. Second, it policed the female body, for instance, outlawing the miniskirts of the 1960s with a decree that skirt length had to be at the knee. And third, it made Pinochet's wife, Lucia Iriarte de Pinochet, a spokesperson for the military state; she advocated family values within what she called the "moral Christian home" and continually invoked the father's place as head of the household (Pratt 1999, 21). However, the state could not achieve its rhetoric of retraditionalization with defined gender roles within the family structure. In other words, it could not reconcile the triangle of patriarchy, nation, and heterosexual family bonds and values within a regularized context of disappearance, torture, and political murder especially targeted at male revolutionary subjects. In the wake of state violence, the heteronormative, two-parent family structure simply does not exist, since thousands of widows and fatherless subjects were produced. Political dissent in the street pointed out this disconnection and more broadly challenged dominant gender regimes through a large feminist movement inspired by Julieta Kirkwood, a renowned feminist activist and scholar with a strong foothold in the broader human rights and civil rights movements. Kirkwood addresses how second-wave feminist consciousness in Chile arose because state authoritarianism made other kinds of authoritarianism painfully visible (1986).[15]

In *Fernando ha vuelto*, the tropes of gender, both during the dictatorship and in the return to democracy, are expressed through particular scenes and characters that are emblematic of the nation in the transition to democracy.[16] During the dictatorship, especially during the 1980s, women's agency and visibility were extremely high in the public sphere through human rights movements,[17] sex education and liberation, and "feminine" focused organizations, such as soup kitchens and communal centers.[18] After the return to democracy, however, there was a notable decline in mobilization efforts, perhaps due to the fact that there was no longer one (patriarchal) enemy to unify against.[19] At the same time, as Francine Masiello suggests, the aesthetic realm continues to be an important avenue for the re-creations and representations of gender regimes (2001). By looking at the operations of gender in *Fernando ha vuelto* we get a picture of how the military, a hypermasculine institution, is the predominant perpetuator of violence. Critical to this exercise is the necessity to explore how democratic transitions condition gendered subjectivities, such as the roles of the mother, the wife/partner in couple relationships, and sons and daughters. In short, gender analyses and critique unmasks the dictatorship project and its persistence into democracy as a structuring process with gendered outcomes.

What is interesting to note is the disjuncture and distance between discourses of the family in the nation and the lived experience of families under structural conditions of terror. As an institution, the family was the site of conservative politics, forming the foundational blocks of the nation state. National unity has always been conceived as working through male bonds, exemplified by a favorite Pinochet slogan, "Chile, a country of brothers" (Loveman and Lira 1999, 29). The rhetoric of unity between a "country of brothers" naturalized the move between patriarchal family authoritarianism to patriarchal national authoritarianism, and in the process discursively marked female subjectivity in normative ways.[20] While this quote refers to a paternal understanding of the nation, it also underscores the pact among male citizens and the bonds of patriarchy. The language of unity formed the underlying ideological framework of the dictatorship, which naturalized the interplay between the authoritarianism found in the patriarchal family and that found on the national level. As Rosa Linda Fregoso reports, "Feminist critics of U.S. Third World nationalism have argued that male privilege and hegemony derive their force from a reluctance to contest the 'idealized notion' of a monolithic community and, by extension, 'the family romance upon which this notion of community relies'" (2001b, 91).

The family is the site where gender norms are reconstituted; as mothers, daughters, and sisters are empowered through their personal loss, they move the private into the realm of the social. For instance, the women of the Agrupación de Familiares de Detenidos Desaparecidos, whose family members were disappeared, hold press conferences, organize community events, and raise awareness within Chile about the plight of survivors and their families in the democratic transition period. While those who have disappeared provide the impetus for this politicization process, the social spaces of the family and the extended community of the AFDD, in rearticulating the state's closed definition of family, ensure resistance to forgetting and oblivion. Although the persistent effects of trauma can mediate against this effort, communities of affinity and emotional connection are formed, bearing social witness to the existential crisis brought on by state violence and acting upon this loss in the public sphere. In this sense, rather than producing closure, *Obstinate Memory* actively engages the hidden narratives of the past to reconstruct the possibility of historical agency in the present.

MEMORY'S OBSTINANCE

Patricio Guzmán's documentary films (*The Battle of Chile*, 1979; *Chile, Obstinate Memory*, 1997; *The Pinochet Case*, 2001; and *Salvador Allende*, 2004) are rooted in the radical tradition of documentary filmmaking in Latin America, especially in the New Latin American Cinema movement, first articulated by Fernando Birri in the 1970s and characterized by the double commitment to artistic innovation and social transformation. Like other artistic interventions, documentary was constituted and coded as a subversive project during the authoritarian period; thus, many films were destroyed and the site of Chile Films, the national film industry, was permanently shut down by the military regime. Furthermore, repression created a mass exodus of filmmakers to other nations, virtually stopping film production in Chile for the duration of Pinochet's reign. Significantly, exiles produced a kind of ideological continuity in modes of production, extending the New Latin American Cinema from the earlier topic of revolution to the later effort of illuminating and constituting a social and cultural field of memory. As Patricio Guzmán explains, "Memory matters. The historical memory of a nation shapes its expectations. It may be terribly painful to speak of terrors and tragedies of the past. But the truth inspires hope, and that inspires the will for social change" (Aufderheide 2002, 25). Like other filmmakers working in this genre, Guzmán produced a film language of social memory with the purpose of reshaping the dictatorship's historical reconstruction of events.[21]

In a central sequence of the film *Obstinate Memory*, a young Carmen Vivanco is recognized in *The Battle of Chile* by an audience of her now elderly Socialist Party counterparts. The filmmaker located the older Carmen Vivanco and films her in real time, in front of a frozen image of herself from the 1970s shown on the television behind her. Off camera Guzmán asks, "Is that you who we see there on the screen?" To which she flatly replies, "I have my doubts." The disturbing moment in the film forces the viewer to ask how it is possible that all these people are able to make this recognition, when she is unable to recognize herself. Guzmán follows the statement by asking her to name the members of her family who have been disappeared. As the list grows before the viewer, she rattles off the full names of five members of her family, including her husband and two sons. The final image, namely, the ghostly superimposition of Carmen Vivanco's earlier black-and-white image over her present image in color, crystallizes for the viewer the encounter with rupture and unimaginable loss. Prior to the disappearance of her five family members, Vivanco was a vibrant activist for social possibility. In the aftermath of her loss, she continues her social activism, but this time as a ghostly shadow of her former self. In this way, we are witness to the powerful separation and dissociation that conditions of disappearance produce, wherein former political subjectivity is transformed into a ghostly past.[22]

What emerges toward the end of the film is a powerful enactment of memory's rupture through gendered figures. First to speak is a young woman who articulates the core political struggle in the 1970s as one in which the people fight like David against the Goliath of U.S. imperialism. A young man moved to tears is a striking representation of someone living in a postmemory paradigm, where memory is always mediated by parents, an older generation, or the media. As he relates, on the day of the military coup he was jumping on the bed, excited that he couldn't go to school. His parents had shielded him from the immense tragedy of September 11, 1973, but as he watched the film, the anguish of that day unfolded around him. We also view the figure of silence through a boyish audience member who does not speak but merely cries; he has a look of utter torment on his face as he watches scenes of military troops rolling into poor communities and brutalizing their members. This boy is not given voice in *Obstinate Memory;* he is rendered only as a mute subject. His silence is for cultural critic Nelly Richard a metaphor for the totality of forgetting in the postdictatorship period (2001). Another way to meditate on the figure of silence is to not assume that silence, as rupture, must always be narrated. Is it only that power mandates this young person's silence, or is this display of the affect of pain a necessary part of the inaccessibility of pain?

Tellingly, it is a male figure who gets the last word in the scene at the end of *Obstinate Memory:* Ernesto Malban, a professor who has served the role as the director's surrogate in earlier film segments. And in a disappointingly hegemonic, masculinist gesture, the professor is compelled to tie up the shards of traumatic memory that have been laid before us when he says, "in that shipwreck I was glad to be a part of it," claiming, or maybe reclaiming, a kind of male revolutionary subjectivity. The desire of the professor and, more importantly, of the filmmaker to produce a universalizing narrative of the experience of the Allende period is actually an expression of the defeat of Allende's revolution. The director, at the end of the film, is moved to assert his own masculinity by redeeming Allende's project within a national context that would rather subsume the socialist experiment.

Furthering a gender analysis of Guzmán's films, *Obstinate Memory* and *The Pinochet Case*, positioned from the transnational space of exile, are both attentive to testimonies of female former prisoners, bringing forth these stories at a time when they were absolutely ignored in the nation. In this sense, the films did important political work (if and when they were shown). At the same time, there is a pattern of reproducing the problematic formulation of woman as victim and sufferer for the nation. That is, Guzmán's subjects narrate for the camera, expressing their suffering without linking their stories to their social activism with groups such as the Agrupación de Familiares de Detenidos Desaparecidos or with the other aspects of their lives. Guzmán unwittingly limits female subjectivity and neglects its social source and agency. Guzmán and Caiozzi both confine their female subjects to a specularity of the graphic details of the encounter with state terrorism, without giving them the power to enunciate what living with this violence looks like. Ultimately this format can access only a predictable pattern of the revelatory gesture, ordering stories of rupture and discontinuity into an economy of ready-made apprehension. In this sense, what does the revelatory gesture block out?

Unlike Carmen Vivanco, a female subject who is portrayed as having been involved in the street battle for civil rights in the nation, Fernando's mother in *Fernando ha vuelto* is captured solely in her identification with the kind of pain and suffering that comes only from having one's son or daughter disappear. Without a sense of finality, the condition of permanent mourning and grief has traumatic consequences on the psychological health of relatives, as Fernando's mother shows. Moreover, for mothers of disappeared children, this loss is perhaps the most painful of all losses. As Robben indicates, "There is something unnatural about a child dying before its parents, especially when it has grown through the fragile stage of infancy into healthy adulthood. The severing of this relation is experienced as the destruction of self, the world, and the meaning of life" (2000, 87). When coupled with the inability to mourn a corpse, this "unnatural" experience produces an extreme psychological state and persistent feeling of rupture that interrupts what is conceived of as normal everyday life. *Fernando ha vuelto* forces the viewer to confront the mother's trauma, empathize with it, and ask oneself about the human cost of extreme violence: How can one bear such pain? Loss becomes a force for introspection for those who remain.

If silence takes many forms, what would another rendition of the fragments of its eruption look like? How could a work resist universalizing the experience of memory or the Allende period or refuse to minimize its own importance through the interpolation of masculinized defeat or the specularity of the testimonial? Marilú Mallet's *La cueca sola* (2003) provides us with some possible responses through Monique Hermosilla, a survivor of the Villa Grimaldi concentration camp. Hermosilla describes how, as an exile in Belgium, she had put all the painful memories of sexual terror into a box that she tucked away somewhere in her mind and then went about her daily business, until one day six years later her body literally collapsed. She got up and collapsed again. Roberta Culbertson discusses how, after violence, the body contains memory that is silenced from recall and narrative possibility because of its unreachable character. As she suggests,

> No experience is more one's own than harm to one's own skin, but none is more locked within that skin, played out within it in actions other than words, in patterns of consciousness below the everyday and the constructions of language. Trapped there, the violation seems to continue in a reverberating present that belies the supposed linearity of

time and the possibility of endings. It at once has a certain
pastness, is a sort of "memory-knowledge" as Mary Warnock
would call it, and is not past, not "memory"—that is, a personal, narrated account of something completed, locatable
in time—at all. Perhaps it is not even remembered, but only
felt as a presence, or perhaps it shapes current events according to its template, itself unrecognized. (1995, 170)

This felt presence is what Hermosilla experiences in the collapsing of the body, and the collapsing of the time-sense of past violation that the body reenacts to bring memories of violence to
the level of consciousness. Hermosilla relates how over a long
period she stitched together the pieces of her life through ther-
apy. In other parts of the film, Mallet indicates that to understand
what it is like to live with torture, terror, and disappearance, one
needs to see how to stitch life back together again, through a
recognition of the body, through political organizing, through
music, through the *cueca sola*—through dancing alone.

In the opening of *La cueca sola* we see four women dressed in
black leotards and skirts, with white handkerchiefs in their hands
against a backdrop of candles. These female bodies enact an experimental rendition of the resemanticized criollo dance, the *cueca
sola*, a dance performed during the Pinochet regime by widows
and other women who danced by themselves to publicly protest
the dictatorship and symbolically denounce the disappearance of
sons, partners, husbands, brothers, and other male figures in these
women's lives. Although in the opening sequence the female
dancers are professionals, later in the film Mallet includes archival
black-and-white documentary footage of women dancing the
cueca sola at a public event, with a public naming of their disappeared male counterparts. Many of the women are coded by dress

and speech as from the working class, one of the core constituencies of Allende's government.

With the soundtrack by singer-songwriter Moyenei Valdés, the first few minutes of the documentary pan over the glossy high-rises of the *barrio alto*, or uptown, the Santiago metropolitan area that has most prospered and grown from the neoliberal economy. Placed against the *cueca sola*, these images of splendor dramatize social inequality in the nation and invoke how poor women bear the greatest burden of authoritarian violence. Moyenei Valdés, whose father, a painter and *brigadista*, was murdered point-blank by the military police while finishing a mural, is shown being interviewed on Radio Tierra, the community radio station that is housed by the organization La Morada, a pivotal site of feminist organizing for the past thirty years. Moreover, Mallet is interviewed by novelist, performance artist, and community radio personality Pedro Lemebel, whose transgressive sexual politics and irreverent practices of the avant-garde produced sustained critiques of Chilean morality, conformity, and the upper classes (Nelson 2002). In chronicles such as *De perlas y cicatrices* (*Of Pearls and Scars*) (1998) and in performance work with the group *Las Yeguas del Apocalipsis* (*The Mares of the Apocalypse*), Lemebel criticized the nation's vast social disparities and the elite classes hypocritical stances on codes of morality, along with their often hegemonic position in support of the dictatorship. Through his multifaceted cultural and intellectual productions, Lemebel's queer politics have consistently made fun of the authoritarian regime and the bourgeoisie in Chile. These references are unmarked in the film but not unknown.

Before us, Mallet connects histories of struggle, histories of communities of affinity, and their ongoing work. The film takes us to the streets to watch activists organizing neighborhoods, discussing health issues with communities, or playing drums. Throughout the film, Mallet highlights Moyenei Valdés, whose Pan-Africanist politics and aesthetics provide a counternarrative in a nation that makes racial heterogeneity invisible. Toward the end of the film, Mallet again follows Valdés, this time to Funas, the militant organization of the daughters, sons, and grandchildren of those who were disappeared and murdered. Within a culture of impunity, members of Funas, following the Escraches carried out by Argentinean youth after the dictatorship in their country, have taken it upon themselves to point out torturers in the streets by marking their houses with red paint, pasting flyers on their neighbors' doors that read, "Do you know that a torturer lives next door to you?" and blowing horns to get public attention where the legal realm has only managed erasure. Through these scenes, the director acknowledges the very complex set of subjectivities and negotiations her subjects enact: we hear and feel testimonies that are embedded in the larger structure of lives. In the opening scene the filmmaker says, "This is the first film I have shot in Chile, my native country, after thirty years of exile. I wanted to tell the stories of certain women whose journeys I witnessed." She tells these stories, but her broader project is to thread the histories of a multiply defined, decentered revolution.

The work of Marilú Mallet focuses on the complex female subjectivities of the postdictatorship, on those who are engaged in the struggle, addressing the psychic, somatic, performative, and activist dimensions of personal trauma. The film is not unique in providing representational space to testimonial voice and narrative, since there are places where this memory dwells, but it is singular for placing the subjects of captivity, torture, and rupture in a larger context and trajectory of lived experiences, of childhood, of music, of living.

DOCUMENTARY FILMS can disrupt silence, bounded experience, and isolation while moving individual traumatic experiences into the realm of collective acknowledgment. Making survivors' stories publicly available in the technological format of documentary unsettles what is known or imagined about the past, and what is silenced or shut down. However, while documentaries have the capacity to interrupt hegemonic processes of forgetting and individuation, they can also reproduce dominant social roles and assumptions. Certain films about memory capture the absence of public dialog about the legacies of violence and the collective importance of these dialogs, especially for the next generation.

The films I discuss in this chapter give representational weight to the spectrum of memory and forgetting during the postdictatorship period and reflect the social and political moment of their production. The central theme in the short film *Fernando ha vuelto* is the endless pain caused by disappearance and its psychological effect on family members who have no body to mourn.[23] Faced with the remains of a skeleton in the film, we are challenged to look squarely at the issue of disappearance. The main concerns of the film resonated with those Chileans who had not yet publicly told their story, at least prior to the forthcoming narratives of torture by tens of thousands of people who spoke for the Valech Report. The film, as Alexander Wilde might have it, helps to erupt public memory (1999).[24]

Through these films, the stories of state terror return to challenge institutional narratives about the past, providing alternative standpoints from which to understand the complex and unending effects of collective trauma and loss in the present. In a personal way, audiences encounter the worlds of those who perished, survivors, and their relatives, where chronological time is both a relative and irrelevant concept. As these images show, pain, suffering, and loss persist.

5

Doubling 9/11

Exile Culture and Activism

> I say to you that I am sure that the seed that we now plant
> in the dignified conscience of thousands and thousands of
> Chileans cannot be definitively buried. They have the power,
> they can smash us, but social processes are not detained, not
> through crimes nor power.
>
> Allende's last words, transmitted by
> Radio Magallanes, September 11, 1973

It has become widely known, although there are still quarters of continuing denial, that after the military coup of September 11, 1973, the ship *Esmeralda* was used as a site of torture and detention while anchored in the port of Valparaíso. This was an ironic move by the military, given the ship's reputation as the pride of the Chilean navy.[1] For many years, the four-mast ship sailed from Chile to various global destinations, including the United States, Canada, and Europe, only to be met by demonstrators who denounced and publicized the ship's dark history of torture. Despite the government's effort to use the vessel as a global diplomatic envoy, among Chilean exiles[2] and other human rights activists *Esmeralda* is called the "floating torture chamber" and represents the unfinished business of dictatorship during political democracy. In June 2006, at the San Diego harbor, one of the last places *Esmeralda* is still able to dock in the United States,[3] several dozen first- and second-generation exiles and immigrants, including Chileans, Argentineans, Mexicans, Ecuadorians, and Uruguayans, gathered together to protest its arrival. The Chilean exile organizers of the event, some of whom were founders of La Peña Cultural Center in Berkeley, had intimate knowledge of this history, since they were former political prisoners and survivors of the Pinochet era. They used the occasion to shine a light on the crevices of memory about torture by handing out informative flyers to those invited to dine aboard *Esmeralda* (fig. 20), holding signs while chanting slogans, and answering questions from tourists.

Much like the iceberg that I introduced in the first chapter, *Esmeralda*, or the Dama Blanca (White Lady), as it is commonly called, is another dense trope of the erasure and attempted purification of Chile's authoritarian past and its legacies. In fact, the nickname "white lady" imagines the ship as a symbol for the national fantasy: chaste, light-skinned, and feminine, devoid of the violence of colonialism, authoritarianism, and patriarchy. However, whereas the traveling iceberg is devoid of historical and social memory, *Esmeralda* and its voyages cannot help but activate memories of state terror. As event organizer Héctor Salgado puts it, "It can hardly go anywhere anymore. Everywhere it travels protestors gather" (pers. comm., June 2, 2006). Its voyages around the world, despite its official mission, spur and consolidate human rights activism by Chilean exiles and other witnesses, by whom it

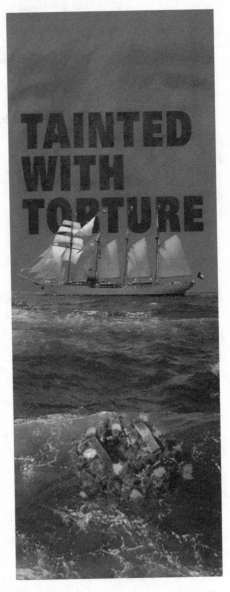

Figure 20. The *Esmeralda* shown on the cover of a pamphlet that resignifies the ship's hegemonic meaning. Image and pamphlet by Guillermo Prado.

is defamed as a global and ethical symbol of shame. *Esmeralda* also serves as a memory symbolic that consolidates political and affective communities in transnational settings, giving life to the memory of torture and feeding the identity of exile.[4] I use the term *affective communities* to follow Ann Cvetkovich, who argues that politics has an affective dimension. For instance, emotions like grief, anger, death, and homophobia fuel the political work of AIDS activism (2003, 157). State terrorism, loss, and displacement spurred meaningful political activism in exiles' new home in the North, helping to keep the memory of the Chilean story within the spotlight for over thirty years.

In this chapter I focus on the representations and activities of those who fled Chile between 1973 and 1989 because of dictatorship repression and threats. Chileans fled to multiple destinations, including other Latin American nations, such as Brazil, Venezuela, Cuba, and especially Mexico, which took in thousands of political exiles. Other nations also accepted them, including Canada, Spain, France, Denmark, Sweden, Germany, and to a lesser degree the United States. Among Chileans, the politics of claiming exile in these locations always incurs the question, "When did you leave?" Isabel Allende, the author of internationally best-selling novels and the niece of Salvador Allende, writes, "If he, or she, says before 1973, it means that person is a rightist and was fleeing Allende's socialism; if he left between 1973 and 1978, you can be sure he is a political refugee; but any time after that, and she may be an 'economic exile,' which is how those who left Chile looking for job opportunities are qualified. It is more difficult to place those who stayed in Chile, partly because those individuals learned to keep their opinions to themselves" (2003,

46–47). My own experience suggests that it is impossible to meet other Chileans living outside the nation without first maneuvering the statuses of political orientation, histories, and class divisions often based on this initial question.

An obvious, though often understated, point is that the United States was not an unproblematic destination for Chilean political exiles. On the one hand, in an effort to detach himself from the human rights record of previous administrations (i.e., Nixon and Ford), President Carter offered official political asylum, but only to four hundred Chilean exile families.[5] Many of these exiles boarded commercial planes, their tickets paid for by religious and human rights organizations. Other families were able to make arrangements through university contacts, church solidarity, and so on. On the other hand, the social democratic orientation in Sweden, Belgium, France, and Denmark created favorable conditions for resettlement in Europe. Caribbean and Latin American nations also opened their doors to large numbers of exiles, some of whom were forced to continue their journey as dictatorships spread in the region (e.g., Argentina in 1976).

Culture and memory are important ways in which the process of exile becomes more than just an expression of deterritorialization or an endless bereavement of the homeland. Rather than emphasize exile as only an experience of rupture, fracture, discontinuity, and isolation, I focus on its possibility for political engagement and social imagination. Diana Taylor describes cultural memory as "a practice, an act of imagination and interconnection" (2003, 82). My research indicates that the structure of understanding and identifying with exiles contributes to important work in the social world, particularly through cultural memory, even though compulsory exile from Chile ended in 1990. I analyze an early documentary by Marilú Mallet entitled *Journal inachevé* (*Unfinished Diary*) (1987) and Patricio Guzmán's *The Pinochet Case* (2001), both exemplary of the condition, perspective, and interactions of exiles. Within the historical context of *peñas* (events by cultural centers), I also discuss an art exhibit and project on the politics of memory titled "Two 9/11s in a Lifetime," an effort organized by a group of Chilean exiles in San Francisco. As sets of social meaning, these political events, cultural sites, and representations expose the afterlife not only of exiles but also of socialism, authoritarianism, interventionist politics, and the unfulfilled political promise of democracy in Chile. On the flip side, these efforts also reveal possibility through a politics that consolidates Latina/o communities in the face of events of rupture and provides continuity to prior social struggles. These collective expressions of cultural memory expand our understanding of democracy by pushing through its often bounded and elite definition. The memory struggles that exiles wage through democratic public culture in transnational arenas have an impact beyond confined notions of what democracy is and can be.

DOCUMENTING EXILE

Documentary was an important way to communicate political ideas and capture a revolution in motion, although filmmakers were targets of repression in Chile. As denouncements of authoritarianism and bearers of historical memory, documentaries were much more likely to be made, aired, distributed, and viewed outside the nation.[6] Director Marilú Mallet's *Journal inachevé* (1982) best represents the genre through a very personal and gendered take on exile that emphasizes psychological dislocation, cul-

tural disjuncture, and, strikingly, the continuity of cultural practices that are reconstituted in the new location.

In contrast to the denunciatory Marxist language and the
wider vantage point of other films of the time, Mallet's more personal approach to the dramatic effects of transition centers on her
own often difficult inhabitancy of exile. In *Journal inachevé* she
documents the cultural and racial divisions in Canada between her
social world and that of her Australian husband, documentary director Michael Rubbo. Throughout the film Mallet aligns herself
with immigrant and working-class issues, with scenes of a Chilean
exile on the verge of deportation hearings and of her interviews
with a Latin American female factory worker, which reveal Mallet's affiliations to a political project that continued despite the
death of Allende. Rubbo is set up opposite these portrayals as a
powerful white male figure and cultural producer who makes demands on Mallet to be "more direct and purposeful" in her filmmaking. The culture and gender clash premise leads to two very
powerful scenes where they perform before the camera the beginnings of their break-up, culminating in a direct address where
Rubbo says, "Now we're probably going to get a divorce."

Mallet's film is autobiographic and performative, documenting her life and her uneasy transition to Quebec.[7] Quebec's cold,
snowy winter, which forces indoor and presumably individuated
living, becomes a metaphor for her transition. A group of Chilean
friends gathers in her home, drinking red wine and eating em-
panadas while delivering *payas*, the folkloric call-and-response
rhymes of the Chilean *campo*. The gathering, with guitar music
by Mallet's brother on the soundtrack, is filmed in one take, which
works to illustrate the affect of collective exilic spaces. These

scenes are familiar to the Chilean identity in exile, reminiscent of the *peña*, the cherished space of sociability. Of course, in showing such scenes there is a danger of reproducing dominant stereotypes of Latin Americans as always gathering around food, drink, and comedic relief, while pining for their lost homeland. However, Mallet effectively problematizes the purity of nostalgia and difference such scenes produce by calling attention to cultural conflict. For instance, Mallet's young son, Nicolas, speaks in French and shows his inability to understand Spanish, while Mallet's husband responds to the dialogs in English. Immediately following this scene, at the film's climax, Rubbo asks that Mallet explain what it is she is trying to accomplish in the film, accusing her of supposedly missing important documentary material, such as Nicolas's dislocation within her Chilean social world. Rubbo's insistence on molding Mallet's film becomes an expression of protective and even condescending masculinity, masked by his anxiousness for Mallet's integration. Indeed, Mallet's responds to Rubbo's obtuse questioning by criticizing his desire for linear, conventional Western storytelling. The film's work in such scenes underscores how domestic space, a supposed site of familiarity, is actually crisscrossed with the contradictions of exilic loss, nostalgia, language, displacement, and gender hierarchies. The theme of nostalgia is further expressed through the recurring figure of a man playing an accordion, bringing to mind images of the circus and childhood, and symbolizing the collective loss of innocence (fall of Allende) and the individual loss of nation (condition of exile).

As in other exilic productions, testimonial in this film is a mechanism for communicating loss. In Mallet's film Salvador Allende's daughter, Chilean congress member Isabel Allende, tells a powerful story about the last time she saw her father in La Moneda Palace, narrating how lucid he was during a time of preeminent national crisis. The scene is interwoven with footage of the bombing of the presidential palace and archival footage of Isabel Allende's public denouncement of her father's death. But unlike other productions of that moment, the film places a decided focus on female subjectivity and perspective of dictatorship and exile, showing the personal and devastating consequences of authoritarianism for a high-profile daughter. Later, as if to contrast the narration of these matters by Allende and to offer another female perspective, the camera centers on Mallet's mother in silence, smoking a cigarette while making artwork about the four generals who orchestrated the military coup.

The work of Mallet's film, then, is to emphasize gendered articulations of loss and survival that are connected through the cartography of exile, specifically in the location of Quebec, Canada. Through Mallet's film we are faced with the regime of terror, the social, economic, cultural, and psychological dislocation that it created, and the racial and gendered realities left in its wake. In fact, the film immerses us in the uneven and messy experience of living in exile or, as Amy Kaminsky puts it, *after* exile, in the process of continuing to identify with and feel the effects of the forced separation that produces "otherness" (1999).

EXILE IRRUPTIONS

It would be difficult to argue that the drama that unfolded during Pinochet's arrest was not the prototypical "irruption of memory" that Alexander Wilde famously theorizes (1999). In fact, it seems that the media event of global proportions actually came to define the postdictatorship period, even though, as my interviewees told me, the political impact on national human rights efforts was minimal in the short term.[8] After decades of impunity, Pinochet's arrest was the culmination of many legal maneuvers, social movement efforts, and a series of twists. In fact, the astounding arrest and detention of Pinochet on October 17, 1998, happened only because of the indictment by Spanish magistrate Baltasar Garzón that attempted to extradite Pinochet from London to Spain. In September, feeling quite comfortable in his political immunity, the ex-dictator was in London on a pleasure trip and had tea with Margaret Thatcher. During the trip he experienced back pain and underwent surgery at a clinic in London. When he awoke from surgery, he was arrested by the London police.

The day was memorable for many Chileans around the globe, sparking impromptu celebrations and gatherings of exile communities in cities everywhere. The arrest marked the international stripping of Pinochet's immunity, where he was legally issued a provisional warrant alleging that he was responsible for the murders of Spanish citizens during his reign as head of state. Five days later, Pinochet was served with a second warrant, which widened the allegations to include "systematic acts in Chile and other countries of murder, torture, 'disappearance,' illegal detention and forcible transfers" (Amnesty International 1998). He ultimately was sent back to Chile, where he was later arrested and released several times until his death on December 10, 2006. Throughout the world, this series of events catapulted human rights movements and fueled debates on the question of impunity for dictators such as Pinochet, with far-reaching national and global consequences.[9]

By narrating and constituting exiles' historical agency, Patricio Guzmán's films helped spur efforts toward democratic openings and a deepening of democracy beyond the nation.[10] His film *The Pinochet Case* witnesses the personal and social explosion that Pinochet's arrest produced. The main narrative thread is the chronological explanation of the events leading up to Pinochet's arrest, his attempted extradition to Spain, and its legal and political aftermath. As if to contrast the voluminous false discourses propagated by Pinochet and his supporters, the documentary mounts its evidence against Pinochet and his dictatorship at a deliberately slow and meditative pace. The most powerful narratives in the documentary explore the conditions of state terror, while recalling the Allende period. The film emphasizes testimonials from exiles and survivors and shows scenes of social activism on the streets of London and Santiago. Banging on drums and chanting slogans from an earlier era, protestors stained their hands with red paint to symbolize the blood of the dictatorship and wrapped their heads in black cloth to represent the state's use of torture. Here, the connection between Chilean communities around the world and their identification with the Allende period and its legacies through the survival of exiles, relatives of those who were disappeared, and torture victims is tantamount to the ethical location of the film and its impact on film audiences. In fact, Patricio Guzmán's films, like other documentaries that thematize atrocity, call upon international human rights networks, circuits, and actors to make visible their versions of history.

The Pinochet Case was shown on British television and screened at different venues across Europe and the United States, including at the 2002 Human Rights Watch International Film Festival in London and New York, winning numerous international prizes.[11] These public spheres gave Guzmán, human rights organizations, and Chilean activists access to sympathetic audiences, who are both potential makers of collective action and likely channels of material resources. Significantly, the viewer witnesses the shared political commitments that extend from Chile's Pacific to Europe's Atlantic oceans. Through street protests that use drums, banners, and slogans from the Allende period, along with theater and puppets, this community of affinity crosses national spaces. The role of exiles in Guzmán's film is especially revelatory, as there has often been a perception that exiles did not bear the burden of dictatorship because of their absence. While there is compassion among some Chileans for the struggles over identity that the children of exiles have confronted, resentment is sometimes directed at those who are seen to have "abandoned" the country and the political struggle against dictatorship.[12] The perception of abandoning the cause stems from the fact that at the time of the military coup few imagined its seventeen-year duration and the capacity of the military regime to sustain authoritarian control, and many exiles left at the beginning of the Pinochet regime, hoping to soon return.

Of course, the stereotypes of exiles were and continue to be a mythology about the Other, myths that Guzmán addresses in the film, although somewhat indirectly. For instance, positive images of Chilean exiles in London gathering outside the clinic where Pinochet was arrested in an effort to make the issues visible show explicit commitment to the political project of making the dictatorship accountable for its crimes. Scenes such as these illustrate an emotional connection to the historical outcome of the dictatorship that some generations of exiles continue to identify with, even after almost three decades of physical separation from Chile.[13] The performative gathering of groups of survivors, filmed as they entered the room and assembled and later shown in a series of still shots, echoes scenes in Gillo Pontecorvo's famous film *Battle of Algiers* (1966). The camera pauses on each face with the sound track in silence, moving slowly to make the next survivor visible in the scene. Silence in these shots forces the viewer to absorb the suffering and loss of survivors and imagine their daily survival.

These scenes are juxtaposed not only with the intimate portraits of victims and survivors but also with vibrant street scenes where the spectacle of death and torture is invoked by social activists, a move that reveals the stakes of empty legal rhetoric. Bodies marched in downtown Santiago with their heads *encapuchadas*, covered by black cloth with rope tied around the base of the neck. The covered heads represent the dictatorship's torture techniques, specialized practices that were exercised in concentration camps and torture chambers throughout the 1970s. The protestors' choices are startling, heightening the dramatic elements of torture during Pinochet's reign. As the narrator says, "In Santiago, impatient with the slowness of the judicial process, groups of young people organized to denounce, in their own terms, the ex-torturers and the professionals responsible for the repression who are still holding high positions." At a rally we see groups of young people, and through a bullhorn one shouts, "On this anniversary of the police force of Chile, we have come to salute Espartaco Salas Mercado, the institution's Director of Intelligence. Salas Mercado joined the DINA in 1974 and participated in the operations of this criminal association to detain, torture, assassinate, and make disappear hundreds of Chileans. He is now the police director of intelligence, appointed by the former president Eduardo Frei and ratified by Ricardo Lagos." Through scenes like these, the film works within the oppositions of reality versus superficiality, suggesting that the story of veracity, justice, and memory is told in the street rather than within institutions of power and written precedents. In fact, young people take justice into their own hands and effectively "out" torturers, work that the democratic Chilean state and other government entities have been more reluctant to do.

The scenes in the film work to unpack the misperceptions of Chilean exile communities; they also connect witnesses across nations to show the persistence of activism in the aftermath of dictatorship. In this way, the film registers cultural memory and agency across transnational spaces, contributing to social activism on issues of violence, its unresolved legal character, and its tenacious hold on minds and hearts. What Guzmán captures is both a national and global perspective, filming in London, Santiago, and Madrid to create an audiovisual archive of a transnational irruption of memory.[14] Guzmán's film shows a rich and vibrant human rights effort in London and Santiago, and the complex persisting traumatic effects. By revealing the personal and collective effects of authoritarianism, *The Pinochet Case* shows how these effects play out in exile as a form of continuity of political ideals and practices.

When the Chilean government argued that Pinochet's detention could bring instability to the nation, informed activists and Chilean exile communities knew that justice could not be carried out in Chile. The nation's long history of injustice and the multiple layers of institutional barriers, such as constitutional changes and constraints in amnesty laws, implied that Pinochet would still not be prosecuted. Therefore, the maneuvers by the transition government to have Pinochet returned were mere threats and empty rhetoric, seen by some survivor organizations as political ploys. On the other hand, the possibility of Pinochet being tried away from Chile provided real hope of a prosecution.

"TWO 9/11s IN A LIFETIME"

Like documentary film, another important site of expressive Chilean public culture that carried over into exile was the *peña*, which had its roots in rural popular cultural gatherings and was given urban visibility by the great Chilean folksinger and composer Violeta Parra. During the Allende years, the *peña* was transformed into important collective gathering spaces where aesthetics and politics commingled in truly interdisciplinary environments. The Bay Area has been a significant site of continuing the *peña* tradition, particularly through La Peña Cultural Center in Berkeley, founded by Chilean exiles, many of whom were members of the Movimiento de Izquierda Revolucionaria, MIR (Revolutionary Left Movement), during the Allende period and later survived political imprisonment in concentration camps such as Villa Grimaldi, Puchuncaví, and Tres Álamos. As the center's Web site states, "Exiles brought to the U.S. their memories and the cultural experiences of having created gathering places for communal art. Thus, La Peña became an imagined country for them as it welcomed this community in diaspora." This political work continues in exile through cultural events and fundraisers aimed at raising awareness of and solidarity with the struggles of the political Left. The center's scope expanded from its initial focus of the repression in Chile as Venezuelans, Mexicans, Cubans, African

Americans, Chicana/os, and Asian Americans played an important role in the planning and execution of the myriad events that have taken place there. In short, the trajectory of La Peña as a cultural political project can be mapped onto local, national, and international Left political struggles.

Another important precursor to the center was the art group Colectivo Acciones de Arte, CADA (Collective of Art Actions). Created in 1979, CADA encompassed an artistic movement during the Pinochet years that interrupted the hegemony of authoritarianism through ephemeral performances and acts. A connection to CADA, although not consciously intended by the organizers, was noted by many audience members who viewed La Peña's art exhibit called "Two 9/11s in a Lifetime: A Project and Exhibit on the Politics of Memory." The exhibit connected the military attack on September 11, 1973, in Chile with the militarized attack of September 11, 2001, in United States. The exhibit was created by the 9/11 Collective, a group of nine Chileans including myself, who as the daughters and sons of Chilean exiles, identify as exiles with ties to both nations.[15]

In one large area within the halls of the New College of California, the 9/11 Collective divided the space so that each artist's work was hanging on the walls or displayed as installations on the ground. Color and black-and-white photographs, acrylic and oil paintings, and objects of daily use were organized around the long walls of the room, and dozens of chairs were set up before a podium at the front of the space. In one corner of the room, a large piece of paper was hung, beckoning audience members to detail their impressions of the exhibit and their own versions of the politics of memory. The premise of the project and art exhibit, shown for two weeks during September 2003 in the Mission District in San Francisco, was the concept of dialog, particularly about the meaning and irony of living through or dealing with the effects of two 9/11s during the life span of one person. The move to connect two dates through expressive culture, across historical timescapes and geopolitical locations, reflected the social location of many U.S.-based Chilean exiles, who had lived through both dates. For the most part the main organizers of the exhibit were not directly victimized by the military dictatorship, but they had been socialized within the context of exile and the traumatic effects of political violence that deeply impacted their parents, grandparents, and other family members. This second generation of Chilean exiles came of age in the United States with strong emotional, familial, and political bonds to the traumatic memories of their parents' generation and stories.

During conversations in the organizing process, we thought it would be important to show ourselves as the 9/11 Collective. After numerous debates about how to best do this, we decided to orchestrate a group activity for the opening night of the art exhibit. After an introduction, readings from writers, a video, and a short lecture, the house lights of the Cultural Room of the New College dimmed in preparation for the closing performance. Clad in black and carrying candles, we walked to the front of a diverse audience of three hundred people. Roberto Leni Olivares, a member of the collective, wanted to "create a space where we could name those we wanted to remember, people who tried to make things better and paid dearly for their commitments." Taking turns, we announced a name or group and the audience responded with a period of silence and then applause. I felt compelled to commemorate Carmen Rojas, who, as I discuss in chapter 2, was held captive from 1974–1977 at the Villa Grimaldi and Tres Álamos concentration camps and suffered torture and sexual violence at the hands of the DINA.

We then turned to the audience and asked, "Who would you like to commemorate?" For a minute there was silence, and then we asked the question again, this time more forcefully: "Who would you like to commemorate?" Slowly, audience members began to stand and state the name of a person or group that had experienced the oppression of terror and its afterlife. Victims of the World Trade Center attacks and those who were disappeared in Pinochet's Chile were among the first to be named. As the voices gained momentum, people began to stand up simultaneously. In fact, in a very moving response over the next hour, audience members stood and spoke, commemorating Salvadoran civil war victims, Guatemalan genocide casualties, "political prisoners everywhere," "Mapuche victims of dictatorship and economic development projects," and, more personally, local activists who had since passed away.[16] The process of publicly naming and thus linking victims and activists from around the Americas produced a connected memory about seemingly disparate events. Afterward, many audience members congratulated us for the event, stating how moved they were by the interactive memorial.

In many ways, the performative act by the 9/11 Collective was a form of cultural memory, enacting the terror imaginary of dictatorship and other forms of systematic violence. It also was an astounding instance of public improvisation; what began as testimony by sons and daughters of exiles was transformed into an embodied scenario of political alliances across national and historical experiences. This participatory performance, where dozens of audience members gave public witness, made it possible to link the personal and collective levels of terror, dislocation, and its concomitant resistance. The social identities of different generations of exiles produced by political violence activated relevant and meaningful cultural memory with other social groups.

The cultural production and experience of the 9/11 Collective illustrates the complex workings and reworkings of exile identity in the United States, especially for a second generation of Chileans, whose relationship to dictatorship violence is, for the most part, indirect. For instance, Álvaro Lagos's photographs of dictatorship brutality were placed next to photographs of San Francisco police beating a group of antiwar protestors. In both images the lens captures the viewpoint of the subject being beaten, emphasizing the violence of power from above. Painted in fluorescent orange, red, and green, Pancho Pescador's "El otro América," incorporates images of EZLN (Zapatista) indigenous struggles and Pinochet marchers within a neoliberal landscape, where everything is on sale. The writers, photographers, and visual artists in the 9/11 Collective display a wide range of knowledge about politics in Latin America, the United States, and other parts of the world. For this younger generation, the experiences among Latina/o communities and the process of identifying with one's own Chilean history serves as the basis for ethnic and political identification in the United States. At the same time, the members of the 9/11 Collective resist claiming one national identity, seeing themselves instead as exiles with at least two national reference points.[17]

The experience of the 9/11 Collective suggests that groups of exiles and immigrants with experience of terror and displacement have the opportunity to draw upon these histories in their host countries to create new cultural imaginaries. Not only Chileans, but also Salvadorans, Nicaraguans, Guatemalans, Argentines, and so on, have embattled national histories of violence and rupture that are bound to U.S. policies of intervention and the subsequent geopolitics of forgetting. Within the United States, these experiences can produce transnational political subjectivities and identifications that facilitate dialog and coalition-building with other similarly located populations. Nationality is not a static identity that is unchanged by a new environment; in fact, for many Chilean exiles and immigrants, the United States transforms their notion of *Chilenidad*. As an act of rewriting national tragedy, the 9/11 Collective situated Chile's military coup of September 11, 1973, as the object of narratives about cultural expression and commemoration. The particular combination of exiles' experience (produced out of state terror in both Chile and the United States) and its cultural and strategic use by a group of second-generation Chilean exiles offered a space for reflection, dialog, and witness to an unforgettable date.

EXILES, AND THEIR daughters and sons, continue to be informed by the memory of violence and its institutional politics. This focus is important because the transnational significance of Allende's death and Pinochet's dictatorship has had deep resonance for many on the political Left and has produced a wide net of international solidarity in its wake.[18] Exiles have historically offered spaces where connections between U.S. interventionist policies, authoritarianism, and their personal effects can be made in ways that also offer material and emotional refuge to its participants. Thus, the exilic experience has very much shaped the political landscape of the

Latin American diaspora and the broader histories of struggle. In this way, this historical period has informed social identities that are activated through cultural memory. These registers form a transnational memoryscape of politics, identity, and cultural production that is reactivated and rearticulated in an effort to deepen the contours of democracy beyond its limited geopolitical and elite definition.

Rivers of Memory

Something long anticipated, yet shocking, happened as I was finishing a draft of this book, an end to a story without endings. General Augusto Pinochet died of a heart attack while under house arrest in Santiago. Pinochet died a disgraced former dictator, under house arrest a half dozen times in London and in Santiago, with his bank accounts frozen, his wife charged with fraud and theft of government monies, and his offspring threatened with legal prosecutions as they traveled to Miami and other global destinations. He died discredited, as commentators around the world have indicated, although impunity for his systematic violation of human rights was still not totally lifted.

When a friend phoned me with the news of Pinochet's death, it was not possible for me to take the next plane to Chile or even to drive a few hours to La Peña Cultural Center in Berkeley, my home away from my permanent home in Los Angeles. I did not anticipate my reaction. A curious thing happened. Where anxiety over the pressures of academic life, publication deadlines, and endless demands had been lodged within me, something new emerged—hope, a sense of ease, even the possibility of momentary freedom. Indeed, like other second-generation exiles and countless other identities formed out of rupture, I have no memory that is not framed by Pinochet, a history that has structured me to acquire knowledge and move toward action on Central American intervention, U.S. racism, and the global consequences of the politics of "national security."

Much of what prompted my search for nation, memory, and the past was the desire for a route out of memory toward a momentary, then finally sustained, fulfilled break from the problems that we need continually, and impossibly, to reform. Perhaps this is what torture survivor Guillermo Núñez already knows. He realizes, for instance, that transitional states of democracy, as in exclusionary nation-states, reinstate and often amplify historical inequalities rather than provide forms of social justice that, in Hartman's formulation, re-member (1997). This knowledge moves us to the question of redress, which like re-membering goes beyond the call for symbolic and material compensation for the past. Redress means creating equitable, just, and constructive social relations, in whose absence memory is continually elided and deformed.

In Southern Cone democracies, where judicial processes have been slow, uneven, or deficient, the role of cultural memory takes on great significance by offering new ways to imagine the past en route and linked to the future. Those who remember and memorialize are engaged in the act of making democracy, addressing its vulnerabilities in ways that ultimately strengthen its foundation. The exercise of cultural citizenship at the Villa Grimaldi Peace Park, in documentaries by Patricio Guzmán and Silvio Caiozzi, in the art of Guillermo Núñez, and at the "Two 9/11s in a Lifetime" exhibit consists of inhabited forms of memory. Memory operates through gatherings, mourning, collective witnessing, remembrance, intergenerational dialog, and historical understanding of what occurred, enlivening the practices of democracy.

One of the objectives of my book has been to draw out the complexities regarding issues of memory within postdictatorship Chile, especially in terms of the persistence of state violence in the lived subjectivities of dictatorship victims. I have privileged the domain of representations precisely because they are meaningful and multifaceted sites that produce practices of cultural memory in the social field. Rather than mere repositories of memory, these sites offer symbols, testimonies, architectural spaces, images, and narrations of witness about state violence within Chile's public sphere. In addition, they structure and delimit the ways that democracy has failed to account for certain kinds of experiences, including the dramatic military counterrevolution, with grave human consequences. I have attempted to engage with the poetics and symbolic gestures that representation produces to approximate an unrepresentable reality. My other persistent concern has been to elucidate the shortcomings of the contemporary project of democracy in Chile by filling in the terror imaginary.

I approach the traces of the past through multiple sources, places, and people to disarticulate the impact of hegemony's denial of the human debris. These sources show the public/private tensions, elisions, and complex subjectivities that emerge from a fragmented social and political landscape of violence. The ethical dimension of writing in and through the fragments, the social organization of survival, and the ongoing political practices casts the nation's remaking of itself as an amnesiac and obliviating performance.

In the book *La batalla de la memoria* (The Battle of Memory), a social history of Chile in the twentieth century, María Angélica Illanes positions cultural battles over memory as key access points to history. For Illanes, the current cultural battle around memory and forgetting was born out of the profound social trauma left by military power. In Illanes's words, "The cultural battle for memory is, it seems, the political road towards a democratic future" (2002, 13). Illanes believes that the increased circulation of cultural work about the violent past helps accelerate the conditions for democratic openings and the deepening of democracy, an argument that my work in this book evidences.

The long process of dealing with the atrocities of the past has, of course, not been unique to Chile, whose lessons and contradictions draw parallels with the authoritarian legacies of Spain, a transverse historical route that returns us to the shadow side of icebergs, colonial spectacles, and the location of Pinochet's attempted extradition. Concerning the decades following the Spanish civil war, Paul Preston has said, "The transition to democracy . . . was a transaction between moderates of the Franco regime and moderates of the democratic opposition, and part of the negotiated transition was that there wouldn't be any digging up of the past. Spain never held any trials for officials of the dictatorship" (Kolbert 2003). Spain took more than seventy years to begin to recover the memories of dictatorship and to unearth the past; the process of recovering memory began only after the death of Franco in the 1970s. As in Chile, the remaking of the Spanish democratic nation forced preemptive closure on the past, along with its ongoing reopening.

What I offer is a mode of inquiry that sustains its focus on effects as the unending legacy of violence, where representation makes historical gnosis tenable through cultural indexes. Put another way, analyzing cultural memory within a field of power has helped me understand the persistence of memory in the social imaginary and its hold over people's lives. It is both the site of passage to the other world where those who were disappeared still whisper their final words to loved ones and the place where locating bones provides a liberating moment of ritual closure. Cultural memory coheres as a format for the continual odyssey that exiles, returnees, torture victims, and those fighting for dignity are forced to undertake. In all these ways, representations express the complexity and subjectivities of living with the presence of the past.

Although Lagos's administration consolidated efforts toward symbolic and material incorporation, efforts that Bachelet's administration has continued in the current period, memory refuses to be tamed. Whereas during the authoritarian period and the beginning of the transition period, the primary political modality was refusal, producing all kinds of social silences about the past, the current configuration simultaneously proliferates and fractures social memory. Again, the memory of political violence refuses to be tamed, while the national and global scene is littered with dictatorship's unfinished business. I hope I have shown the moral and ethical imperative that state terror produced in the nation's move toward neoliberalism, democracy, and economic globalization. Representations prove to be productive and nuanced sites for encountering individual, family, community, and social responses that resist incorporation into hegemonic projects of memory and forgetting. Instead, victims and allies counteract the pressure of closure with fluid cultural and political practices, aesthetic representations that bear witness and heed advice about future directions.

Figure 21. The Mapocho River, June 22, 2005. Photo by Nicole Hayward.

I end my story with the Mapocho River (fig. 21), which runs the length of Santiago like a wet spine and continues to be a meaningful emblem of cultural memory today. It was the place that ran red with the blood of so many victims, where bloated bodies had to be fished out of the water by passersby during the first days of the military coup. At first the river was channeled to allow for the expansion of the capital city. Now it has been further constrained by the construction of an underground freeway that runs directly to Santiago's *barrio alto*, the wealthy neighborhoods, instead of to the poor peripheral urban communities. The containment is a symbol of neoliberal democracy, but the river, like the entanglements of so many memory symbolics, is impossible to fully tame. During the construction of the freeway on a cold, rain-drenched day in 2002, I watched on my television screen as the Mapocho burst open the concrete walls, spilling out to flood the construction areas and taking with it several machines. Memories of violence, like the river in winter, indeed have the capacity to burst through the forms of their containment.

NOTES

CHAPTER 1

1. Aníbal Quijano originally developed the term *coloniality of power* (1997b), which Mignolo describes as "a conflict of knowledges and structures of power" that "presupposes the colonial difference as its condition of possibility and as the legitimacy for the subalternization of knowledges and structures of power" (2000, 16).

2. The notion of branding nations is by now a familiar tactic of marketing plans. "Nation Brands of the 21st Century" (Anholt 1998) was among the first on this topic in the advertising world. In a more critical vein, scholars Marita Sturken and Sarah Banet-Weiser in a panel entitled "Consumer Citizenship and the Making of National and Transnational Values" (2006) analyzed how U.S. companies and products worked to cast the nation as triumphant and unified in the aftermath of 9/11/01, thereby remaking the nation through consumption solidarity.

3. The neoliberal economic model was put into place by the Chicago Boys, a group of Chilean technocrats, most of whom attended the Pontifical Catholic University of Chile and then studied economics with Milton Freidman at the University of Chicago. They restructured the Chilean economy during the Pinochet regime according to two phases:

in the early 1970s, the group concentrated on "monetary and macro-economic stabilization policies," and in the later 1970s the focus was much more on the "expansion of neoliberal policies to other spheres of society" (Valenzuela 1995, 55).

4. I use the term *political democracy* to signify its classic political science definition as representative democracy, the liberal system of rule "embracing elected 'officers' who undertake to 'represent' the interests of 'rule of law'" (Held 1995, 5). This definition also follows that of Guillermo O'Donnell (1992, 51), who cites Roberto Dahl to state that for polyarchy (political democracy) to exist "all full citizens must have unimpaired opportunities: 1) to formulate their preferences; 2) to signify their preferences to their fellow citizens and the government by individual and collective action; 3) to have their preferences weighed equally in the conduct of the government, that is weighted with no discrimination because of the content or source of the preference" (1971, 2).

5. I use the terms *political democracy* and *democracy* interchangeably. It is significant for Chile and other nations that political democracy began to be defined through economic planning only in the post–Bretton Woods period. That is, in the aftermath of World War II, the notion of political democracy and capitalist economy became deeply imbricated in their definitions. From Keynes (1936) forward, economic planning rather than other forms of human capital was seen as the main agency of development (Arjomand 2004, 329).

6. Rebranding, I would contend, is a form of nationalism that provides an ideological structure for social relations to adhere to, give allegiance to, and participate in political bureaucratic regimes of democracy, wherein commodity culture penetrates the workings of the state, including the production of *market citizens* (Leiva 2005, Banet-Weiser 2007). Thus, the term *democratic capitalism*, rather than *political democracy*, is perhaps a more apt description of state formation.

7. "The spectacular state" is for Agamben that which empties out the possibility for communicability itself (the absolute evacuation of language as social cohesion) through a "society of spectacle where capitalism has reached its extreme figure" (2000, 75, 84–85).

8. Oren Baruch Stier has a useful conceptualization of memory forms as desires, whether they be personal quests for narratives to alleviate burdens or yearnings for identity from the second generation of survivors and others. The memory forms are transmitted as ritual and traditional mythos, as nostalgia, and as art and artifice. My own take especially highlights representation (art and artifice), which Stier describes as "the creative construction of a relationship to the past built out of the intensely felt desire for that relationship. Such creativity calls attention to the crucial fact that memory is about the presentation and representation of past events, not the events themselves" (2003, 2).

9. There are instances as well where the state has made official memory out of counter or alternative memory. This has been especially true of Michelle Bachelet's government, which I discuss briefly in a subsequent section. For instance, the 2006 opening of the Salvador Allende Museum, sponsored by Bachelet's government, is a dramatic instance of the state reinscribing the memory of the Allende period into official memory. The museum of modern art dedicated to the memory of Allende is located in downtown Santiago. Notably, the museum's director is José Balmes, a famous painter on themes of the dictatorship and military coup. The building's architect was Miguel Lawner, whose illustrations and books on captivity have been critical to representing experiences of torture and imprisonment that leave no visual record.

10. I also want to acknowledge the various forms of violence, where interlocking systems of oppression can produce less visible violence, such as racism, classism, and sexism, which may have immediate damaging effects on bodies or can have slower, accumulative effects that may be just as consequential (see Gilmore 2002; and Gordon 1997, 2007). Of course, literary and cultural critics also point to epistemological violence in the construction of histories and the production of knowledge. In this book, I am specifically referring to the effects of state terrorism on bodies and subjectivities, effects that stem from a bureaucratic, organized, and state-sponsored system of political violence.

11. Robben and Suárez-Orozco's *Cultures under Siege: Collective Violence and Trauma* provides helpful theoretical models for my study. The

book focuses on the ways that societies deal with the bodily, psychic, and sociocultural changes produced by large-scale violence, and how cultures affected by massive outbreaks of violence deal with their legacies.

12. Spillman examines how meaning-making processes occur "on the ground," "in the institutional field," and "in the text." A focus on meaning making "in the text" draws on insights from the humanities more than from sociology. In this way, "cultural repertories, objects, and texts are analytically distinguished from their social contexts and treated as independent objects of inquiry" (2005, 8). One of my epistemological claims is that objects and texts can often function to constitute social contexts, most clearly in the use of public spaces like memorials. That is, textual sites not only exist as independent sites of meaning making but constitute social meanings as well (see chapters 2, 3, and 4). There is, I believe, an important conversation that needs to continue within the discipline of sociology, acknowledging how the methodologies of humanities can enhance, rather than diminish, sociological inquiry.

13. Although I have chosen here not to pursue the notion of cultural politics, this is a rich area of inquiry and understanding of culture and practice. In particular, Herman Gray's book *Cultural Moves: African Americans and the Politics of Representation*, discusses the structuring practices of representation and counterhegemonic aesthetics through the idea of a cultural formation (2005, 15–18).

14. I conducted research at the Fundación Allende at the Casa Herrera site. See Louis Bickford's excellent article "Human Rights Archives and Research on Historical Memory: Argentina, Chile, and Uruguay" (2000) for an extended review of archives in the Southern Cone.

15. This site contains memorials to those murdered, including Father Juan Alsina, who was murdered there on September 19, 1973; fourteen townspeople from Puente Alto who were murdered on October 12, 1973; and five priests killed during the dictatorship.

16. I thank sociologist John Brown Childs for his insight that site work rather than fieldwork can help us navigate out of the modern trap that constructs hierarchies about what counts as evidence and archival materials when conducting research. One can travel somewhere, thereby "le-

gitimizing" the venture, to conduct site work, but it is not a necessary condition.

17. *Revista de Crítica Cultural*, Editorial Cuarto Propio, and Universidad Arcis have been especially important in publishing on such topics.

18. La Peña Cultural Center, located in Berkeley near the Oakland border, was founded by Chilean exiles in the late 1970s. This space has adapted, not always easily, to shifting political times and local, national, regional, and global issues, as multiracial and generational considerations have put pressure on and have become incorporated into the cultural and political mission.

19. Although the notion of an imagined community has been groundbreaking for understanding the role of print capitalism in the forging of nation, Anderson's work, as many have commented, fails to consider how the "deep, horizontal comradeship" he describes (1991, 7) does not apply uniformly to all national subjects.

20. For Agamben, the primordial figure of this exclusion is the refugee, while for scholar Etienne Balibar exclusions are constituted through the "rights of man" in "the modern dialectic of equality and freedom" (Balibar 1994, 39).

21. Commenting on the construction of European nations in the eighteenth and nineteenth centuries, Hardt and Negri state that the "identity of the people was constructed on an imaginary plane that hid and/or eliminated differences, and this corresponded on the practical plane to racial subordination and social purification" (2000, 103).

22. For a richly textured account of working-class organization in the industrial sector and how the revolution was propelled forward, see Winn 1989.

23. For a classic discussion of Chile's history that puts Allende's government into a larger context, see Loveman 2001. The most recent edition includes analysis of the nation's democratic transition period.

24. See the introduction to David L. Eng and David Kazanjian's *Loss: The Politics of Mourning* (2003) for an incisive discussion of the relationship between loss, melancholia, and their expression.

25. Fernando Leiva offers a useful exposition of the process of eco-

nomic restructuring in Chile, identifying three periods of the Concertación, or transition government, to discuss the shift from "domination to hegemony" during the transition period, beginning in 1990. He classifies the periods of the Concertación government as I, II, and III, which correspond to (1) Aylwin's challenge of governability (1990–1995), (2) Frei's challenge of sacralizing the market (1995–2000), and (3) Lagos's challenge of producing legitimacy (2000–2006). He also tracks the trajectory of the emergent social discourses of "citizen participation," "civil society," and "need to draw upon the 'social capital' of the poor" as ones that aim to prop social support for open markets during the transition (2005, 83–87).

26. The point here, as Menjívar and Rodríguez carefully address, is not to make a reductive argument that U.S. hegemony was responsible for all cases of political violence in the region but rather to use case studies to "indicate a clear and persistent pattern of U.S. influence over the political violence conducted by Latin American states" (2005, 4–5).

27. Stier's reference to the multiple shoes conveying the multiplicity of loss is taken from a longer passage by *Time-Life* correspondent Richard Lauterback, who visited a "shoe warehouse" at the Nazi death camp Majdanek in Poland. Stier suggests that such icons were in place in the early journalistic narratives of liberation (2003, 30).

28. See Barbie Zelizer's *Remembering to Forget* for an important discussion of the photographic images of war atrocity and their metonymic representation of the Holocaust (1998).

29. See the introduction (especially 7–12) to Gordon's *Ghostly Matters* (1997) for a detailed description of his concept of ghostly matters, its relationship to sociology, and how it intervenes in questions regarding representation.

30. The term *transition* itself assumes that the passage from one kind of state to something completely new is discontinuous. It is often conceived as an eventful rupture rather than a sign of economic and political stability.

31. See Eviatar Zerubavel 2006 for a wonderful discussion of silence and its figuration as a public secret.

32. For a very skillful review of Western and non-Western conceptual framings of trauma as the dialectic of individual and collective memory, see Saunders and Aghaie 2005. Historian James Young, writing on the Jewish Holocaust, describes how memorials are representations of the past that impact the present through their signification and social meaning (1993). Barbie Zelizer argues that visual representations translate "some aspect of the Holocaust into another code by which it can be made differently meaningful" (2001b, 2). In her analyses of art and monuments, Zelizer understands how visual and cultural sites about events like the Holocaust use a range of genres and codes to make meaning in conditions that are impossible to narrate and represent. Rosa Linda Fregoso, in elaborating on Lourdes Portillo's documentary approach, makes a similar point. She shows how social realism and the realm of the imaginative can work to conjure and unsettle unrepresentable events (2001a).

33. See Stern 2004 for an interesting and innovative discussion of classifications of memory in the context of postdictatorship Chile.

34. *Crear poder popular* was Allende's Popular Unity government slogan for building people's power.

35. It is contested as to whether President Salvador Allende committed suicide or was killed. In both cases, he was forced to his death at the hands of the military.

36. In a meeting with the CIA on Chile, Richard Nixon famously ordered the agency to "make the economy scream" (declassified CIA notes, Sept. 15, 1970).

37. See Steve Stern's book on memory for an explanation of how these events have different meanings and memory formations for the political Right and other social groups in the nation (2004).

38. During the first years of the dictatorship, Milton Freedman's vision was carried out by the Chicago Boys. High rates of economic growth were celebrated as an economic success story within the international sphere. During this period, General Pinochet and his advisors opened the gates to the international market, receiving a flood of imported products and reorienting the national market toward exports. From 1990 for-

ward, when democratically elected President Aylwin took office, free market policies continue to dominate the political and economic agenda.

39. See Lisa Yoneyama for a brilliant exposition on how scholars such as Susan Buck-Morss and Jürgen Habermas adopt Benjaminan dialectics of history to rethink conventional historiography and the reconstruction of memory as a future-oriented project with a "radical orientation toward the past" (1999, 30–31).

40. Like many longtime possessors of green cards in the United States, I decided to take the practical step of becoming a citizen after September 11, 2001. The bureaucratic process took until 2006 for reasons I still do not fully understand; however, I received my U.S. passport the day after Pinochet's death, coupling two strange, yet somehow strangely liberating, experiences.

41. With the economic shifts and increased social gaps and demands of the late 1960s, dependency theory and import substitution industrialization based out of CEPAL (Comisión Económica para América Latina y el Caribe, or Economic Commission for Latin America and the Caribbean) in Santiago were an important focus of U.S.-based Latin American studies. Of course, Area Studies itself was created out of the Cold War as a way to manage and potentially subdue "the South." During the Allende period, thousands of scholars, activists, and other interested parties traveled to Chile to experience (or help curtail) the social and economic revolution, making the post-Allende period a decisive focus of much scholarship that aimed to understand, analyze, and critique authoritarianism.

42. For detailed discussions of the history of Richard Nixon, Henry Kissinger, and U.S. involvement in supporting the military coup in Chile, see Peter Kornbluh's *The Pinochet File: A Declassified Dossier on Atrocity and Accountability* (2003).

43. By using the term *different* I am referring to the kind of historical knowledge that is produced by "silenced societies." This term is used by Abdelkebir Khatibi, an Arab/Islamic thinker who discusses societies in which knowledge production proliferates but is not taken into account within the larger "planetary production of knowledge." See Walter

Mignolo's discussion of knowledge production and circulation, and his analysis of Khatibi's work (2000, 71).

44. For an excellent discussion of this topic, see Portales's study on democratic transition (2000).

45. Puchuncaví and Chacabuco in the north of the country and the Venda Sexy (Sexy Blindfold), Londres 38, and José Domingo Cañas in Santiago are a few examples of torture centers that were completely decimated or whose properties were sold and transformed. In Argentina and Uruguay some sites are being preserved. My point here is to underscore how most places suffer erasure in the effort by militaries to eliminate all evidentiary traces.

46. On this point there is an excellent and rich bibliography, which includes Tomás Moulian's *Chile actual: Anatomía de un mito* (Chile Today: Anatomy of a Myth) (1997) and Nelly Richard's *Residuos y metáforas* (Remains and Metaphors) (1998).

CHAPTER 2

1. The following account is from my field notes on June 12, 2002 (late autumn in the Southern Hemisphere).

2. I am referring to Jeffrey C. Alexander's too brief comments on the role of Southern Cone literature that analyzes memorials as "efforts to memorialize the victims of the repression" in order "to restore the objective reality of the brutal events, to separate them from the unconscious distortions of memory" (2004, 8). He critiques the literature as a form of lay trauma theory.

3. This information is based on five research trips to Villa Grimaldi during 2001, 2002, and 2005; ethnographic research; interviews; and material from numerous archives. As I observed during my last trip, some of the sites of torture had been rebuilt and developed.

4. Literally the term *roto* means broken, but it is also a pejorative term used by the elite to describe the popular classes.

5. See Gordon 2006 for a discussion of how secretive military prisons, and their emergence in public social consciousness through photo-

graphs, are historically linked to lynchings of black men and women between the 1880s and the 1930s.

6. Many doctors broke the Hippocratic oath by participating in torture scenes and sexual violation, whose psychological effects and staging are the central themes in Chilean author Ariel Dorfman's *Death and the Maiden* (1991), a novel and play that was later dramatized on film by the director Roman Polanski (1994).

7. The Valech Report, or the National Commission on Political Imprisonment and Torture Report, constructs categories of torture methods where many of the typologies of torture I describe in this chapter are also detailed.

8. Unless otherwise noted, all translations are my own.

9. The Web site has since undergone dramatic changes; it is now also in German and English, and features many images of the site, as well as many more navigable spaces and options. These changes reflect the international human rights community's increased interest in the site over the last couple of years and the committee's move to give its work at the Peace Park an international dimension.

10. Luz Arce's story is considered the primary testimonial of imprisonment at Villa Grimaldi. See Marcia Alejandra Merino's film *La flaca Alejandra* (The Skinny Alejandra) (1991) for Arce's testimony of the process of her betrayal to MIR during captivity. Arce's narrative of betrayal, shame, and guilt, to the dismay of some former prisoners, became a focus of attention and controversy in the aftermath of the military dictatorship, when *La flaca Alejandra* circulated in human rights festivals. Also see the important testimonial *The Inferno: A Story of Terror and Survival in Chile* (Arce 2004), which contains Arce's involvement with MIR, her capture by DINA, and her subsequent collaboration with DINA under physical pressure (2004). In comparison to the distribution of the documentary, there are few copies of Rojas's story in circulation. It is, however, an important narrative to analyze, both because of its insight into the experiences of the female captive and because of the personal and political journey that is revealing of that historical period.

11. Avery Gordon refers here to the genre of nonnaturalist fiction by

South American women writers, particularly the work of Luisa Valenzuela (1979), that considers how and why we tolerate violence. Carmen Rojas's testimonial (ca. 1981), although of a different genre, demands a similar ethical accountability. Ariel Dorfman's play *Death and the Maiden* (1991) uncovers the psychological bonds of the afterlife of torture through a female captive's revenge on her torturer, a physician.

12. I am not suggesting that female revolutionaries were on egalitarian footing with their male counterparts. However, revolutionary processes had opened up this possibility, which was then effectively shut down on the bodies of female captives. For an interesting comparative narrative of women as revolutionary bridges see Shayne 2004.

13. It is important to mention that there are famous cases where female captives did break down and tell their stories and became state confidants and agents. This is another form of agency, although a negative form that allowed for better treatment of these women captives. Under such historical conditions, it is impossible to untangle the "truth" of what occurred, even though there are clear judgments made against such women (and men) by other former prisoners. Many were drugged, beaten, and threatened with death, making their betrayals hardly acts of free volition.

14. In informal conversations with Chilean ex-prisoners I have heard this oft-repeated sentiment.

15. For an astute and complex analysis of the conditions and limitations of representation and the possibility of revolutionary male subjectivity, see Saldaña-Portillo 2003.

16. *I, Rigoberta Menchú* is a notable and well-known example. Although a political narrative and Menchú's agency are both encoded in the text, the international intention behind the text's circulation and the expectations of its audience preclude the presence of a detailed political analysis unencumbered by the desire to produce affective attachment and solidarity in the reader.

17. For an important discussion of the broader problems and pitfalls of promoting human rights, see David Kennedy's book on the topic (2004).

18. I put the term in quotes since it is not a foregone conclusion that Chile is an economic success. While it is certainly true that Chile has improved its economic position in front of the global economy, and that the market economy has brought gains to some, it is also plausible the neoliberalism has increased the gap between rich and poor. See Winn 2004.

19. It is important to acknowledge how these dreams were encased within a developmentalist paradigm. See Saldaña-Portillo's poignant discussion of how revolutionary subjectivity did not escape the developmentalist regime of subjection, most pointedly because of its reaction to the logic of the age of development (2005).

20. Obviously, the comparison of Villa Grimaldi to places such as Auschwitz suffers from problems of size, purpose, and scale of extermination. Even so, the important affective elements that provide the visitor with a connection to the past at Auschwitz are decidedly missing at Villa Grimaldi. There is no access to clothes, torture machines, or other remnants.

21. I thank Steve J. Stern for this insightful comment about the subtleties of interacting with the memorial.

22. The transition government had promised a third phase of construction, but it ultimately was truncated and renegotiated without much input from the community of relatives of the disappeared (Díaz, interview with the author, April 19, 2002).

CHAPTER 3

1. Macul is an area where many land takeovers and struggles over landownership took place during the 1960s and 1970s.

2. I use this aspect of Scarry's definition of torture throughout this chapter.

3. See Barrera 1998 for a very good overview of the process of economic restructuring under both the authoritarian and the transition governments.

4. "The Miracle of Chile," now commonly referred to as "the Chilean

Miracle" in the mainstream press, was a term coined by Milton Friedman to describe Pinochet's support for economic liberalization with dramatic social and economic consequences.

5. See Cavanaugh 1998 for a discussion of how the state imagines torture as a method not only over the social body but over the soul itself. He goes on to discuss the state's strategy of visibility and invisibility as a "[religious] imaginative drama" in conflict with the Christian faith, because of the state's refusal to produce visible bodies, thereby "denying it the possibility of martyrs," necessary to the Christian idea of sacrifice (58).

6. For a visual and narrative review of the plethora of cultural efforts from 1960 forward, see Richard 2004.

7. In my time with Guillermo Núñez, he repeatedly denoted his artistic expression as social commitment. Ironically, contemporary Chilean revolutionary discourses that warned of the danger of falling prey to cultural imperialism did little to change the U.S. pop art influence on Núñez's art. Also see Dorfman and Mattelart 1984.

8. In these early denouncements there seems to be a dialog with the art of José Balmes, a recognized Chilean abstract painter who also conveyed the experience of terror. Balmes's work on Chilean terror is well known in the country, and he appears in Patricio Guzmán's film *Obstinate Memory* (1997). One of his recurring images is a shovel against a backdrop of Chile's flag (to depict the work of unearthing bodies from mass graves); he also paints images based on photographs from the military coup. The two artists found each other as exiles in France and exhibited their work together in multiple venues.

9. Núñez corroborates the suggestion that his art was understood in Europe, particularly in France, by saying that he was "well received there" (interview with the author, March 12, 2002). Again, there was a connection between Núñez's positive reception and Leftist politics, as François Mitterrand was in power at the time, and student mobilizations peaked. In the eyes of the French Left, Allende's government and the massive social movements of the time were important social projects whose exiles were exalted as national heroes.

10. Another possibility is that he was marginalized within the ranks

of those who viewed exiles as lacking the courage and strength of those who stayed. Of course, this latter position was a move to deny that many people were forced to become political exiles.

11. For a discussion of this genre, see Gooding 2001. To place Núñez's work in the context of twentieth-century Chilean art, see Ortega 2000.

12. On the operations of invisibility and hypervisibility, see Gordon 1997. One important recent case of hypervisibility and torture emerges from the hegemonic media channels' circulation of photographs from Abu Ghraib that reproduce, for instance, the nameless and faceless subjects of U.S. state and military violence. Citing Ralph Ellison's comments in the *Invisible Man* about the African American male subject, Gordon argues that hypervisibility is often an alibi for invisibility (1997, 16–17).

13. Judith Herman traces the genealogy of the term *constriction* back to Pierre Janet, who theorized about posttraumatic amnesia (1997, 45).

14. For comments about how the methodology in Chile and other nations unfolded, see Lira and Arestivo 1994 and Lira and Castillo 1991.

15. I use the term *rebrand* intentionally here to point out how new narratives of nation are not made purely through national exigencies of reconstruction but are also reconstituted through consumer capitalism's expansion.

16. This latter effort happened in 1998 only after Pinochet's London arrest, when the democratic government was eager to bring Pinochet back to Chile and publicize that it could take care of human rights business itself, a point many critics doubted. The National Roundtable was the conversation between members of the human rights community, the government, and the military, a national process that failed to clarify the whereabouts of many disappeared bodies.

17. This three-volume, two-thousand page report was the culmination of the work of the National Commission for Truth and Reconciliation. On the day of the report's presentation, President Aylwin formally apologized to the relatives of the victims for disappearance. The subject of torture was a notable absence.

18. See Portales 2000, ch. 4, for an important discussion of the pacts between political parties.

19. At the same time, the Valech Report was never tied to juridical prosecutions, and the only officials to retreat on its findings were members of the judiciary branch. In fact, the day after the Valech Report was released, the president of the Supreme Court, Marcos Libedniksy, claimed there was "no credible evidence" and "that distinguished magistrates could have conspired with third parties to allow for unlawful detentions, torture, kidnappings, and murders" (Kornbluh 2005).

20. To cite one famous example, Diamela Eltit and poet Raúl Zurita staged a performance where Zurita used acid on his face and body to show the body as the metonymic site of social erosion and political gain by the Right, with torture as its central strategy.

21. See Ortega 2000 on the art of this period.

22. Here, I am reminded of the success stories of elite politicians of the Concertación Party, many of whom, like Núñez, were exiled to the United States and Europe and returned to be recognized as national leaders of democracy. Unlike Núñez, however, these mostly male returned exiles distanced themselves from public renditions of the violent past, instead serving as key brokers to negotiate pacts of silence about torture.

23. Of course, an important difference is that the liberation of Nazi concentration camps resulted in a massive political campaign of exposure, while in Chile and other Latin American nations burying the atrocities was politically expedient.

24. María Angélica Illanes cites this quote in her book, although she does not name the deputy she saw on television. The original Spanish quote is "debemos pedir perdón por no haber creído en la propiedad privada ni en el mercado" (2002, 15).

CHAPTER 4

1. Jeffrey R. Middents notes how Guzmán filmed *Obstinate Memory* semiclandestinely. He was not the first to return and film this way in Chile; Miguel Littín shot *Acta general de Chile* (General Report from Chile) (1986), which was also documented by Gabriel García Márquez (1986).

2. *The Battle of Chile* is now available as a trilogy in many retail locations.

3. Nelly Richard (2001) has a similar reading about this figure of muteness, although she reads it as a direct indication of the inarticulation of loss rather than as the embodiment of silence with political possibility, a point I later develop. Susana Kaiser (2005) works to fill in the gray areas of the memory of the second generation and their knowledge and understanding of Argentinean state terror and the widespread practice of disappearance.

4. For a classic treatment of this genre, see the introduction to Burton 1986.

5. Gaines builds on Linda Williams's discussion (1995, 4) of three genres that "make the body do things (horror makes you scream, melodrama makes you cry, and porn makes you 'come')."

6. Antonious C. G. M. Robben makes this point in regard to Argentina, but it can also be applied to the Chilean context of disappearance (2000, 87).

7. Agave Díaz had worked with Caiozzi as an administrator. When she was given an appointment to go to the Centro Médico Legal to make an identification through the evidence, she asked Caiozzi if he would accompany her, and as he put it, "he happened to bring along a camera to see what would happen." After filming that day he returned with three more people, one sound technician and two camerapersons, to film the scene with Fernando's family and his remains (Caiozzi, interview with the author, April 11, 2002).

8. It is worth noting that Caiozzi kept suggesting that the film was actually released much earlier, and that we had to pause our discussion about audiences for a minute and work out the dates of its release until he realized that in fact his film came about the same time as the arrest and was shown only in its aftermath. Thus audience members' reactions should be read within this temporal and political framework.

9. Francine Masiello's *The Art of Transition* opens with a discussion of the most powerful scene in the documentary's narrative: that of the first viewing of Fernando's skeleton (2001, 1).

10. I thank Steve J. Stern for pointing out shifts in the identification of remains, especially in the case of Fernando Olivares Mori (see Stern

2009 for a discussion of the Medical Legal Institute's unfinished business in regard to mistaken identifications). In the coda, Agave Díaz speaks about the humiliation of finding Fernando and burying him, only to become uncertain once more that the remains are really his.

11. The title of the section, "The Wait," is symbolic for relatives of the disappeared and victims of the dictatorship, since their ongoing wait with institutions of justice has lasted beyond thirty years.

12. It is plausible to conceive of the anger and loss for these young men within a framework of ongoing present-day social activism. Indeed, Mauricio, in a later scene in the film, is one of the pallbearers of his father's casket, and he also holds a banner for the Socialist Party. This is a tentative conclusion, however, since an analysis of Mauricio's political activism needs to be discussed within the broader terrain of youth activism in Chile, a complex issue.

13. As in Argentina, with the political organizing work of Mothers of the Disappeared, the subjectivities of woman and mother were cast as harmless by the military dictatorship within the public sphere. Patriarchy constructed women as passive citizens, which opened public and political space for women's activism against dictatorship. In other words, the cultural work of patriarchy could not conjure mothers as political agents. Therefore, women organizing around their identities of mother, sister, and daughter functioned to subvert masculine codes of appropriate gendered behavior (see Arditti 1999; Filc 1997; Agosín 1993; Fisher 1989). For a discussion of the important film *Las Madres: The Mothers of the Plaza de Mayo*, see Fregoso 2001a.

14. See Stacey 1996 for a discussion on the family and conservative values.

15. Also see Ríos Tobar 2003 for excellent insight into the broader history of feminism in the context of socialist efforts.

16. Cynthia Enloe's insight that militarization is an incremental process "by which a person or a thing gradually comes to be controlled by the military or comes to depend for its well-being on militaristic ideas" (2000, 3) is true for society as well, and perhaps also exponentially applicable in situations where the military is the state, such as authoritarianism.

17. Human rights movements include multiple efforts, such as the groups that formed among family members of the disappeared (which I address in the next section); La Morada (a women's organization with a series of projects on women); organizations that promoted alternative development and gay and lesbian rights; and women who were prominent in the cultural arts, especially poetry, experimental performance, and public performance.

18. Perhaps the best-known of these examples is the *olla común* (common pot), a cooking cooperative organized by women in poor sectors to meet food needs. See Paley 2001 for a detailed history of women's organizing within marginalized communities.

19. In interviews I conducted in 1996 for a research project on women's social movements, this was an oft-cited explanation given for the decline in visible social movements in Chile.

20. Moreover, as Mary Pratt says, "Pinochet gave direction to women about their 'mission as women and mothers'" whose work was "to defend and transmit spiritual values, serve as a moderating element . . . educate and instill consciousness and conscience, and serve as repositories of national traditions" (1999, 22).

21. I am using Paul Connerton's very useful distinction between social memory as a specific daily practice of reconstituting memory, and historical reconstruction, the wider activity in which social memory is embedded (1989, 13–21). This genre includes such titles as Silvio Caiozzi's *Fernando ha vuelto* (1998); Guzmán's films (1997, 2001, 2004); and Marilú Mallet's two films, *Journal inachevé* (Unfinished Diary) (1986) and *La cueca sola* (2003).

22. While I have little evidence from interviews and ethnography, it seems that some of the social ties between relatives of the disappeared would have already been in place prior to the dictatorship through political organizing. After all, during the Allende period there were tight social relations among and between political units (e.g., party affiliations), members of which were the targets of dictatorship repression.

23. This is one of the reasons it was shown at the forty-first International Congress of Psychoanalysis in 1999 (which took place in Chile).

24. See Wilde's article (1999) for an early scholarly discussion of the eruption of public memory in Chile.

CHAPTER 5

1. The four-mast, steel-hulled *Esmeralda* is considered to be a tribute to the ship that was sunk in the infamous Battle of Iquique, in which national military hero Arturo Prat was ultimately killed. For details of what happened aboard the *Esmeralda* during the dictatorship, see Westphal's article (2003), which documents the abuses and areas of the ship that were used for torture.

2. While there are many important uses of the term *exile*, I discuss the material, psychological, and affective dimensions of exile and its process after compulsory exile has finished. I follow Amy Kaminsky's narrow definition of an exile as one who must contend with "forced separation and a politically construed place of origin whose governing institutions have the ability to impose that separation" (1999, 22).

3. Since 1974, when protestors turned away the ship from the San Francisco Bay, there have been numerous protests, most famously the 1986 bicentennial celebration of the Statue of Liberty, when the U.S. Senate passed a resolution that prevented the *Esmeralda* from participating (Bradley 2002). I attended the protest gathering in June 2006.

4. The production and persistence of the category Chilean exile in the United States may even be more pronounced as a form of disidentification from hegemonic and historically interventionist politics. On the politics of disidentification in the context of queer communities of color, see José Esteban Muñoz's classic work (1999). The irony of living in the United States as an exile is not a small subject, as I discuss, albeit briefly, in the second part of the chapter.

5. In unpublished personal notes written before his death, Chilean exile Hugo Rolando Leni Urbina mentions how this was one of the first times, if not the first, that the United States gave official political asylum to a politically Left-identified social group.

6. An example is *Pinochet: Fascista, asesino, traidor, agente del imperia-*

lismo (Pinochet: Fascist, Assassin, Traitor, and Agent of Imperialism), made in Sweden in 1974 by Sergio Castilla, who chose a film title not known for its subtlety. In the case of historical memory, *Los puños frente al cañon* (Fists before the Cannon) was made in Germany in 1975 by Gastón Ancelovici and Orlando Lübbert and showed the rise of the labor movement during Allende's rule. Jacqueline Mouesca cites these films in her work (1988, 144–45).

7. Canada was the site for thousands of Chilean exiles, and many were granted political asylum.

8. During my fieldwork in Chile throughout several trips, I repeatedly asked interviewees the question: "What change did the arrest of Pinochet and subsequent events produce in Chilean politics?" From all quarters the response was similar: basically after a few months there was no substantial shift in terms of political results or human rights decisions. Only one interviewee, Mireya García, vice president of the Agrupación de Familiares de Detenidos Desaparecidos, had a more nuanced response, describing a more positive judicial outcome in which old cases were reopened and five full-time judges were assigned to human rights cases from the time of the dictatorship. She too had many negative comments about the institutional capacity to forget such a momentous event (presentation and personal communication, Santiago, May 29, 2002). Of course, looking back now and noting the route to Pinochet's arrest and defamation, including multiple accusations, such as those by the former head of the secret police Manuel Contreras, makes it difficult to argue that the attempted extradition did not have a long-term impact on human rights issues in the nation.

9. Of course, the prosecution of Pinochet also had its limits. See Ensalaco 2005 for a discussion of how the attempted prosecution of Pinochet gives insight into the factors that sustain impunity.

10. Guzmán's *The Battle of Chile* (1979) was featured in the 1999 Human Rights Watch International Film Festival, as well as screened at countless solidarity venues internationally throughout the eighties and nineties.

11. Prizes for Guzmán's *The Pinochet Case* were awarded by the Latin American Studies Association (the 2003 Award of Merit in Film), the 2001 Cannes Film Festival (the Semaine de la Critique), the 2002 Amnesty

International Film Festival, and the 2002 Seattle International Film Festival (First Run 2002).

12. I say "sometimes" because it is difficult to pin down sentiments that shift and are reconstituted. However, in numerous informal conversations in Chile and with Chileans in the United States, it is clear that hierarchies of victimization, guilt, and pain exist.

13. It is important to note here that I am referring to large social tendencies and identities, and that the experience of Chileans in exile is actually quite heterogeneous.

14. I am expanding on Alexander Wilde's idea of irruption of memory (1999) to discuss the transnational setting.

15. The members of the 9/11 Collective included Gabriela Cabezas-Fischer, Axel Herrera, Álvaro Lagos, Roberto Leni Olivares, Ariel López, Mabel Negrete, Pancho Pescador (Franz Fischer), Rafasz (Rafael Sanhueza), and myself, all of whom were based in the San Francisco Bay Area at the time. Nicole Hayward, who is Honduran American, was also an integral part of the group and process.

16. Juanita Riloff was a well-known Mission activist that was commemorated at the event. During that evening, as I participated in the performance, I took notes on the events that transpired around me. Thus, I experienced the event as both "insider" and social ethnographer.

17. Katarzyna Marciniak elaborates on transnational exile production and its characteristic resistance to one national category (2003, 66).

18. This is an important subject and beyond the scope of this chapter; however, I will make a few comments to clarify my point. Allende, like other great civil rights leaders, was the repository for global dreams for democracy, social change, and freedom. When he was killed, news of his death reverberated around the world and tattered the dreams that many on the political Left had imagined. As the daughter of a Chilean exile, during my lifetime I have heard hundreds of stories from a very diverse array of people about where they were when they heard that Allende had been killed. They marked this event as an important moment in their lives because of the hope Chile had generated at the time and the despair in the wake of his death.

BIBLIOGRAPHY

Aciman, André, ed. 2001. *Letters of Transit*. New York: New Press.

Agamben, Giorgio. 1998. *Homo Sacer: Sovereign Power and Bare Life*. Trans. Daniel Heller Roazen. Stanford, CA: Stanford University Press.

———. 1999. *Remnants of Auschwitz: The Witness and the Archive*. New York: Zone Books.

———. 2000. *Means without Ends: Notes on Politics*. Minneapolis: University of Minnesota Press.

———. 2005. *State of Exception*. Chicago: University of Chicago Press.

Agosín, Marjorie, and Monica Bruno, eds. 1993. *Surviving Beyond Fear: Women, Children, and Human Rights in Latin America*. New York: White Pine.

Aguilar, Mario. 1999. "The Disappeared: Ritual and Memory in Chile." *The Month: Review of Christian Thought and World Affairs* 32 (12): 472–75.

———. 2000. "El Muro de los Nombres de Villa Grimaldi." *European Review of Latin American and Caribbean Studies* 69 (October): 81–88.

———. 2003. "The Ethnography of the Villa Grimaldi in Pinochet's Chile: From Public Landscape to Secret Detention Centre (1973–

1980)." Paper presented at the Latin American Studies Association conference, Dallas, Texas, March 27–29.

Alarcón, Norma, Caren Kaplan, and Minoo Moallem. 1999. *Between Woman and Nation: Nationalisms, Transnational Feminisms, and the State.* Durham, NC: Duke University Press.

Alexander, Jeffrey C. 2004. "Toward a Theory of Cultural Trauma." In *Cultural Trauma and Collective Identity*, ed. Jeffrey C. Alexander, Ron Eyerman, Bernhard Giesen, Neil J. Smelser, and Piotr Sztompka, 1–30. Berkeley: University of California Press.

Allende, Isabel. 2003. *My Invented Country: A Nostalgic Journey through Chile.* Trans. Margaret Sayers Peden. New York: HarperCollins.

Amnesty International. 1987. *Chile: 50 Cases of Torture, Update II.* London: International Secretariat. September.

———. 1998. *The Absence of Immunity for Crimes against Humanity: Amnesty International Submits Case to the House of Lords.* http://asiapacific.amnesty.org/library/Index/ENGEUR450221998?open&of=ENG-CHL (accessed April 18, 2008).

———. 1999. *United Kingdom: The Case of General Pinochet: Universal Jurisdiction and the Absence of Immunity for Crimes against Humanity.* London: International Secretariat. January.

Anderson, Benedict. 1991. *Imagined Communities: Reflections on the Origin and Spread of Nationalism.* London: Verso.

Anholt, Simon. 1998. "Nation Brands of the Twenty-first Century." *Journal of Brand Management* 5 (6): 395–406.

Anthias, Floya, and Nira Yuval-Davis. 1992. *Racialised Boundaries: Racism and the Community.* London: Routledge.

———, eds. 1999. *Woman-Nation-State.* London: MacMillan.

Appadurai, Arjun. 1996. *Modernity at Large: Cultural Dimensions of Globalization.* Minneapolis: University of Minnesota Press.

Arce, Luz. 2004. *The Inferno: A Story of Terror and Survival in Chile.* Trans. Stacey Alba D. Skar. Madison: University of Wisconsin Press.

Arditti, Rita. 1999. *Searching for Life: The Grandmothers of the Plaza de Mayo and the Disappeared Children of Argentina.* Berkeley: University of California Press.

Arjomand, Said, and Edward A. Tiryakian. 2004. *Rethinking Civilizational Analysis*. London: Sage.

Art Collective. 2001. *Las historias que podemos contar*. Boletin del Parque por la Paz Villa Grimaldi, no. 2. December. Peñalolén, Chile.

Asociación de Abogados por Derechos Humanos en Chile. 1980. *La tortura en el Chile de hoy*. Bulletin 1. November. Santiago, Chile.

Aufderheide, Patricia. 2002. "The Importance of Historical Memory: An Interview with Patricio Guzmán." *Cineaste* 27 (3): 22–25.

Baillard, Georges. 1993. "Imágenes para hoy e, incluso mañana: El juego de la transformación de Guillermo Núñez." In *Retrato hablado: Una retrospectiva*, ed. Guillermo Núñez, 29–32. Santiago: Museo de Arte Contemporáneo, Universidad de Chile.

Bal, Mieke, ed. 1999. *The Practice of Cultural Analysis: Exposing Interdisciplinary Interpretation*. Stanford, CA: Stanford University Press.

Balibar, Etienne. 1994. *Masses, Classes, Ideas: Studies on Politics and Philosophy before and after Marx*. New York: Routledge.

Banet-Weiser, Sarah. 2007. *Kids Rule: Nickelodean and Consumer Citizenship*. Durham, NC: Duke University Press.

Barahona de Brito, Alexandra. 1997. *Human Rights and Democratization in Latin America: Uruguay and Chile*. New York: Oxford University Press.

Barrera, Manuel. 1998. "Macroeconomic Adjustment in Chile and the Politics of the Popular Sectors." *What Kind of Democracy? What Kind of Market? Latin America in the Age of Neoliberalism*, ed. Philip D. Oxhorn and Graciela Ducatenzeiler, 127–49. University Park: Pennsylvania State University Press.

Benavides Escobar, Raúl. 1977. "No existe, ni ha existido campamento de detenidos bajo el nombre de Villa Grimaldi." Ministry of the Interior to the Santiago Criminal Court. Reserved and confidential papers, June 2.

Benezer, Gadi. 1998. "Trauma Signals in Life Stories." *Trauma and Life Stories: International Perspectives*, ed. Kim Lacy Rogers, Selma Leydesdorff, and Graham Dawson, 29–44. New York: Routledge.

Berlant, Lauren. 1991. *The Anatomy of National Fantasy*. Chicago: University of Chicago Press.

————. 1997. *The Queen of America Goes to Washington City: Essays on Sex and Citizenship.* Durham, NC: Duke University Press.

Bhabha, Homi K., ed. 1990. *Nation and Narration.* London: Routledge.

Bickford, Louis. 2000. "Human Rights Archives and Research on Historical Memory: Argentina, Chile, and Uruguay." *Latin American Research Review* 35 (2): 160–82.

Bradley, Michael. 2002. "Grand Ship, Ugly Past." *Sydney Morning Herald,* August 8, 2002. www.smh.com.au/articles/2002/08/07/1028157962906.html (accessed July 6, 2006).

Brown, Wendy. 1995. *States of Injury: Power and Freedom in Late Modernity.* Princeton, NJ: Princeton University Press.

Burbach, Roger, and Paul Cantor. "Teflon Tyrants: After Pinochet, Prosecute Kissinger." Pacific News Service, December, 14, 2004. http://news.pacificnews.org/news/view_article.html?article_id=1951d91231e1373bb86de9ca1e1f8c7c (accessed April 15, 2008).

Burton, Julianne. 1986. *Cinema and Social Change in Latin America: Conversations with Filmmakers.* Austin: University of Texas Press.

Caiozzi, Silvio. 1998. *Fernando ha vuelto.* VHS. Santiago: Andrea Films.

Caruth, Cathy, ed. 1995. *Trauma: Explorations in Memory.* Baltimore: John Hopkins University Press.

————. 1996. *Unclaimed Experience: Trauma, Narrative, and History.* Baltimore: John Hopkins University Press.

Castillo, Carmen. 2003. *La flaca Alejandra.* Digital copy of 35mm. France: INA.

Caucoto, Nelson. 2000. "La abortada Mesa de Diálogo." *Rocinante: arte, cultura, sociedad* 3, no. 20 (June): 16.

Cavanaugh, William T. 1998. "Torture and Disappearance as an Ecclesiological Problem." In *Torture and the Eucharist: Theology, Politics and the Body of Christ,* 21–71. Oxford: Blackwell.

Chatterjee, Partha. 1993. *The Nation and Its Fragments: Colonial and Postcolonial Histories.* Princeton, NJ: Princeton University Press.

Cockcroft, James D., ed. 2000. *Salvador Allende Reader: Chile's Voice of Democracy.* Melbourne: Ocean.

Coffey, Amanda. 1999. *The Ethnographic Self: Fieldwork and the Represen-tation of Identity*. London: Sage.

Colectivo de Arte. 2001. "Boletín del Parque por la Paz Villa Grimaldi." *Art Collective*, no. 2. December.

Collins, Joseph, and John Lear. 1995. *Chile's Free-Market Miracle: A Sec-ond Look*. Oakland, CA: Food First.

Comisión Nacional contra la Tortura. 1989. *Recopilación de documentos in-ternacionales sobre tortura: Convenciones y otros*. Santiago: Comisión Na-cional contra la Tortura.

Comisión Nacional de Verdad y Reconciliación. 1991. *Síntesis del Informe de la Comisión de Verdad y Reconciliación*. Santiago: Comisión Chilena de Derechos Humanos and Centro Ideas.

"Con el excepcional remate de Villa Grimaldi se cierra otra etapa de esta extraordinaria mansión." 1967. *El Mercurio*, November 12.

Connerton, Paul. 1989. *How Societies Remember*. Cambridge: Cambridge University Press.

Coombes, Annie E. 2003. *History after Apartheid: Visual Culture and Pub-lic Memory in a Democratic South Africa*. Durham, NC: Duke Univer-sity Press.

Corporación Parque por la Paz Villa Grimaldi. www.villagrimaldicorp .cl/eng/index_eng.htm (accessed November 28, 2006).

Crysler, C. Greig. 2006. "Violence and Empathy: National Museums and the Spectacle of Society." *TDSR* 17 (11): 19–38.

Culbertson, Roberta. 1995. "Embodied Memory, Transcendence, and Telling: Recounting Trauma, Re-establishing the Self." *New Literary History* 26 (1): 169–95.

Cuprisin, Tim. "Nov. 22 Shaped TV's Role in Writing, Informing Na-tion on September 11." *Milwaukee Journal Sentinel*. November 20.

Cvetkovich, Ann. 2003. *An Archive of Feelings: Trauma, Sexuality, and Les-bian Public Cultures*. Durham, NC: Duke University Press.

Dahl, Roberto. 1971. *Polyarchy: Participation and Opposition*. New Haven, CT: Yale University Press.

Déotte, Jean Louis. 2000. "El arte en la época de la desaparición." In *Po-*

líticas y estéticas de la memoria, ed. Nelly Richard, 149–72. Santiago: Editorial Cuarto Propio.

Dorfman, Ariel. 1984. "The Last September 11th." In *Other Septembers, Many Americas: Selected Provocations 1980–2004.* New York: Seven Stories.

———. 1991. *Death and the Maiden.* New York: Penguin Books.

Dorfman, Ariel, and Armand Mattelart. 1984. *How to Read Donald Duck: Imperialist Ideology in the Disney Comic.* 2nd ed. New York: International General.

Drake, Paul W., and Ivan Jaksic, eds. 1995. *The Struggle for Democracy in Chile.* Lincoln: University of Nebraska Press.

Eltit, Diamela. 1997. "Las dos caras de la Moneda." *Nueva Sociedad* 150 (July–August): 40–45.

Emmison, Michael, and Phillip Smith. 2000. *Researching the Visual: Images, Objects, Contexts and Interactions in Social and Cultural Inquiry.* London: Sage.

Eng, David L., and David Kazanjian, eds. 2003. *Loss: The Politics of Mourning.* Berkeley: University of California Press.

Enloe, Cynthia. 2000. *Maneuvers: The International Politics of Militarizing Women's Lives.* Berkeley: University of California Press.

Ensalaco, Mark. 2005. "Pinochet: A Study in Impunity." In *Democracy in Chile: The Legacy of September 11, 1973*, ed. Silvia Nagy-Zekmi and Fernando Leiva, 116–129. Brighton, UK: Sussex Academic.

"Entrevista a Silvio Caiozzi—Cineasta Autor del Video *Fernando ha vuelto*" in "Chile: Entre la memoria y el olvido." 1999. *ILAS* 1 (2): 16.

Feitlowitz, Marguerite. 1998. *A Lexicon of Terror.* New York: Oxford University Press.

Filc, Judith. 1997. *Entre el parentesco y la política: familia y dictadura, 1976–1983.* Buenos Aires: Editorial Biblos.

First Run Icarus Films. 2002. "*The Pinochet Case:* A Film by Patricio Guzmán." www.frif.com/new2002/pino.html (accessed April 12, 2008).

Fisher, Jo. 1989. *Mothers of the Disappeared,* London: Zed Books.

Flitterman-Lewis, Sandy. 1998. "Terror and Memory in Alain Resnais's *Night and Fog.*" In *Documenting the Documentary: Close Readings of Doc-*

umentary Film and Video, ed. Barry Keith Grant and Jeannette Slo-niowski, 204–22. Detroit: Wayne State University Press.

Fregoso, Rosa Linda. 2001a. "Devils and Ghosts, Mothers and Immi-grants." In *Lourdes Portillo: The Devil Never Sleeps and Other Films*, ed. Rosa Linda Fregoso, 81–101. Austin: University of Texas Press.

———, ed. 2001b. "Introduction: Tracking the Politics of Love." In *Lour-des Portillo: The Devil Never Sleeps and Other Films*, 1–24. Austin: Uni-versity of Texas Press.

Gaines, Jane M. 1999. "Political Mimesis." In *Collecting Visible Evidence*, ed. Jane M. Gaines and Michael Renov, 84–102. Minneapolis: Uni-versity of Minnesota Press.

Garcés, Mario, Pedro Milos, Myriam Olguín, Julio Pinto, María Teresa Ro-jas, and Miguel Larentis Urrutia, eds. 2000. *Memoria para un nuevo siglo: Chile, miradas a la segunda mitad del siglo XX*. Santiago: Lom Ediciones.

García Canclini, Néstor. 1995. *Hybrid Cultures: Strategies for Entering and Leaving Modernity*. Minneapolis: University of Minnesota Press.

———. 2001. *Consumers and Citizens: Globalization and Multicultural Con-flicts*. Minneapolis: University of Minnesota Press.

García Márquez, Gabriel. 1986. *La aventura de Miguel Littín clandestino en Chile*. Bogotá: Editorial Oveja, Negral.

Gilmore, Ruth Wilson. 2002. "Fatal Couplings of Power and Difference: Notes on Racism and Geography." *The Professional Geographer* 54 (1): 15–24.

———. 2007. "Abandonment: Katrina, Prisons and the Politics of In-frastructure." Paper presented at the First Annual Blaut Lecture, As-sociation of American Geographers, April 18.

Gooding, Mel. 2001. *Abstract Art*. Cambridge: Cambridge University Press.

Gómez-Barris, Macarena, and Herman Gray, eds. 2009. *Traces in the So-cial World*. Minneapolis: University of Minnesota Press.

Gordon, Avery F. 1997. *Ghostly Matters: Haunting and the Sociological Imag-ination*. Minneapolis: University of Minnesota Press.

———. 2007. "Abu Ghraib: Imprisonment and the War on Terror." *Race and Class* 48 (1): 42–59.

———. 2009. "The Prisoner's Curse." In *Traces in Social Worlds*, ed. Macarena Gómez-Barris and Herman Gray. Minneapolis: University of Minnesota Press.

Gray, Herman S. 2005. *Cultural Moves: African Americans and the Politics of Representation*. Berkeley: University of California Press.

Guzmán, Jorge. 1993. "Guillermo Núñez, un mestizo ilustre." In *Retrato hablado: Una retrospectiva*, ed. Guillermo Núñez, 13–18. Santiago: Museo de Arte Contemporáneo, Universidad de Chile.

Guzmán, Patricio. 1979 *The Battle of Chile*. Digital copy of 35mm. New York: First Run/Icarus Films.

———. 1998. *Chile, Obstinate Memory*. VHS. Santiago: La Sept Art.

———. 2002. *The Pinochet Case*. VHS. New York: First Run/Icarus Films.

———. 2004. *Salvador Allende*. VHS/DVD. New York: First Run/Icarus Films.

Hale, Charles R. 2004. "Rethinking Indigenous Politics in the Era of the 'Indio Permitido.'" *NACLA* 38 (September): 2.

Hardt, Michael, and Antonio Negri. 2000. *Empire*. Cambridge, MA: Harvard University Press.

Hartman, Saidiya. 1997. *Scenes of Subjection: Terror, Slavery, and Self-Making in Nineteenth-Century America*. New York: Oxford University Press.

Hayden, Dolores. 1995. *The Power of Place: Urban Landscapes as Public History*. Cambridge, MA: MIT Press.

Held, David. 1995. *Democracy and the Global Order: From the Modern State to Cosmopolitan Governance*. Stanford, CA: Stanford University Press.

Herman, Judith. 1997. *Trauma and Recovery: The Aftermath of Violence*. New York: Basic Books.

Hillman, Richard S., John A. Peeler, and Elsa Cardozo Da Silva, eds. 2002. *Democracy and Human Rights in Latin America*. Westport, CT: Praeger.

Hoffman, Eva. 2001. "The New Nomads." In *Letters of Transit*, ed. André Aciman, 35–64. New York: New Press.

Hornstein, Shelley, and Florence Jacobowitz, eds. 2003. *Image and Remembrance: Representation and the Holocaust*. Bloomington: Indiana University Press.

Huyssen, Andreas. 1995. *Twilight Memories: Marking Time in a Culture of Amnesia.* New York: Routledge.

———. 2001. "Of Mice and Mimesis." In *Visual Culture and the Holocaust,* ed. Barbie Zelizer, 28–44. New Brunswick, NJ: Rutgers University Press.

Illanes, Maria Angélica. 2002. *La batalla de la memoria.* Santiago: Grupo Editorial Planeta.

"Informe sobre detenidos: Villa Grimaldi es un lugar donde solo se interroga al detenido, tan pronto es privado de libertad." 1976. *El Mercurio,* March 20.

Irwin-Zarecka, Iwona. 1994. *Frames of Remembrance: The Dynamics of Collective Memory.* New Brunswick, NJ: Transaction.

Jelin, Elizabeth. 2003. *State Repression and the Labors of Memory.* Minneapolis: University of Minnesota Press.

Kaiser, Susana. 2005. *Postmemories of Terror: A New Generation Copes with the Legacy of the Dirty War.* New York: Palgrave Macmillan.

Kaminsky, Amy. 1999. *After Exile: Writing the Latin America Diaspora.* Minneapolis: University of Minnesota Press.

Kaplan, Amy. 2003. "Homeland Insecurities: Transformations of Language and Space." In *September 11 in History: A Watershed Moment?* ed. Mary L. Dudziak, 55–69. Durham, NC: Duke University Press.

Kennedy, David. 2004. *The Dark Sides of Virtue: Reassessing International Humanitarianism.* Princeton, NJ: Princeton University Press.

Keynes, John Maynard. 1936. *The General Theory of Employment, Interest, and Money.* New York: Harcourt Brace.

Kirkwood, Julia. 1986. *Ser política en Chile: Las feministas y los partidos.* Santiago: Facultad Latinoamericana de Ciencias Sociales.

Kolbert, Elizabeth. 2003. "Looking for Lorca." *New Yorker,* December 22.

Kornbluh, Peter. 2003. *The Pinochet File: A Declassified Dossier on Atrocity and Accountability.* Washington DC: National Security Archives.

———. 2005. "Letter from Chile." *The Nation,* January 13.

La Capra, Dominick. 2001. *Writing History, Writing Trauma.* Baltimore: John Hopkins University Press.

Lagos, Ricardo. 2004. "Prologo: Reflexiones y Propuestas." Prologue to *The National Commission on Political Imprisonment and Torture Report (The Valech Report)*, by Sergio Valech, María Luisa Sepúlveda, Miguel Luis Amunátegui, Luciano Fouillioux, José Antonio Gómez, Lucas Sierra, Álvaro Varela, and Elizabeth Lira. Santiago, Chile. November.

Leiva, Fernando. 2005. "From Pinochet's State Terrorism to the 'Politics of Participation.'" In *Democracy in Chile: The Legacy of September 11, 1973*, ed. Silvia Nagy-Zekmi and Fernando Leiva, 73–87. Brighton, UK: Sussex Academic.

Lemebel, Pedro. 1998. *De perlas y cicatrices*. Santiago: Lom Ediciones.

Leni Olivares, Roberto. 2002. "North of a Tree." Unpublished short story. San Francisco, CA.

———. 2003. *Dis-Appeared Words*. San Francisco: 9/11 Collective. Published in conjunction with the exhibit "Two 9/11s in a Lifetime: A Project and Exhibit on the Politics of Memory."

Ley, Ruth. 2001. *Trauma: A Genealogy*. Chicago: University of Chicago Press.

Ley, Samantha. 2002. *British Social Realism: From Documentary to Brit Grit*. London: Wallflower.

Liñero, Germán. 1999. *El Muro de los Nombres*. VHS. Santiago: Área de Cine y Artes Audiovisuales del Consejo Nacional de la Cultura y las Artes.

Lira, Elizabeth. 2000. "Reflexiones sobre memoria y olvido desde una perspectiva psico-histórica." In *Memoria para un nuevo siglo: Chile, miradas a la segunda mitad del siglo XX*, ed. Mario Garcés, Pedro Milos, Myriam Olguín, Julio Pinto, María Teresa Rojas, and Miguel Larentis Urrutia. Santiago: Lom Ediciones.

———. 2001. "Memoria y olvido." In *Volver a la memoria*, ed. Raquel Olea and Olga Grau, 45–60. Santiago: Lom Ediciones.

Lira, Elizabeth, and Carlos Arestivo. 1994. *Psicología y violencia política en América Latina*. Santiago: Ediciones Instituto Latinoamericano de Salud Mental y Derechos Humanos: Ediciones Chile América CESOC.

Lira, Elizabeth, and María Isabel Castillo. 1991. *Psicología de la amenaza política y del miedo*. Santiago: Ediciones Instituto Latinoamericano de Salud Mental y Derechos Humanos.

Littín, Miguel. 1986. *Acta General de Chile/Chile: A General Record*. VHS. Chile: Alfil Uno Cinematográfica.

Loveman, Brian. 2001. *Chile: The Legacy of Hispanic Capitalism*. 3rd ed. New York: Oxford University Press.

Loveman, Brian, and Elizabeth Lira. 1999. *Las suaves cenizas del olvido: Vía chilena de reconciliación política, 1814–1932*. Santiago: Lom Ediciones.

Lyon-Johnson, Kelli. 2005. "Acts of War, Acts of Memory: 'Dead-Body Politics'" in U.S. Latina Novels of the Salvadoran Civil War." *Latino Studies* 3 (2): 205–25.

Las Madres: The Mothers of the Plaza de Mayo. 1985. Directed by Lourdes Portillo and Susana Blaustein Muñoz. San Francisco, CA: Film Arts Foundation.

Mallet, Marilú. 2003. *La cueca sola*. VHS/DVD. Montreal, Canada: National Film Board of Canada.

Marciniak, Katarzyna. 2003. "Transnational Anatomies of Exile and Abjection in Milcho Manchevski's *Before the Rain* (1994)." *Cinema Journal* 43 (1): 63–84.

Masiello, Francine. 2001. *The Art of Transition: Latin American Culture and Neoliberal Crisis*. Durham, NC: Duke University Press.

Matta, Pedro Alejandro. 2000. *Villa Grimaldi, Santiago de Chile: A Visitor's Guide*. Santiago: privately printed.

Mbembe, Achille, and Libby Meintjes. 2003. "Necropolitics." *Public Culture* 15 (1): 11–40.

McCarthy, Mark. 2005. *Ireland's Heritages: Critical Perspectives on Memory and Identity*. Aldershot: Ashgate.

McClintock, Anne, Aamir Mufti, and Ella Shohat, eds. 1997. *Dangerous Liaisons: Gender, Nation and Postcolonial Perspectives*. Minneapolis: University of Minnesota Press.

Meade, Teresa. 2004. "Holding the Junta Accountable: Chile's Tortured 'Sitios de Memoria' and the History of Torture, Disappearance, and

Death." In *Memory and the Impact of Political Transformation in Public Space*, ed. Daniel J. Walkowitz and Lisa Maya Knauer, 191–210. Durham, NC: Duke University Press.

Meller, Patricio. 1996. *Un siglo de economía política chilena (1880–1990)*. Santiago: Editorial Andrés Bello.

Menchú, Rigoberta. 1992. *I, Rigoberta Menchú: An Indian Woman in Guatemala*. New York: Verso.

Menjívar, Cecilia, and Néstor Rodríguez. 2005. *When States Kill: Latin America, the U.S. and Technologies of Terror*. Austin: University of Texas Press.

Middents, Jeffrey R. 2005. "*Me Moría*: Aesthetics, Documentary and the Creation of Nostalgia in Patricio Guzmán's *Chile, memoria obstinada*." In *Democracy in Chile: The Legacy of September 11, 1973*, ed. Silvia Nagy-Zekmi and Fernando Leiva. Brighton, UK: Sussex Academic.

Mignolo, Walter D. 2000. *Local Histories/Global Designs: Coloniality, Subaltern Knowledges, and Border Thinking*. Princeton, NJ: Princeton University Press.

———. 2005. *The Idea of Latin America*. Malden, MA: Blackwell.

Montealegre, Hernán. 2001. "Mesa de diálogo: Impunidad en la medida de lo posible." *Rocinante: arte, cultura, sociedad* 4, no. 28 (February): 31–34.

Montecinos, Verónica. 1998. *Economists, Politics and the State: Chile 1958–1994*. Amsterdam: CEDLA.

Montoya, Roberto, and Daniel Pereyra. 2000. *El Caso Pinochet y la impunidad en América Latina*. La Rioja, Argentina: Editorial Pandemia.

Moreiras, Alberto. 1999. *Tercer espacio: Literatura y duelo en América Latina*. Santiago: Lom Ediciones.

Moten, Fred. 2002. "Black Mo'nin.'" In *Loss: The Politics of Mourning*, ed. David L. Eng and David Kazanjian. Berkeley: University of California Press.

Mouesca, Jacqueline. 1988. *Plano secuencia de la memoria de Chile: Veinticinco años de cine chileno (1960–1985)*. Madrid: Ediciones del Litoral.

Moulian, Tomás. 1997. *Chile actual: Anatomía de un mito*. Santiago: Arcis Universidad, Lom Ediciones.

Mukherjee, Bharati. 1999. "Imagining Homelands." In *Letters of Transit:*

Reflections on Exile, Identity, Language, and Loss, ed. André Aciman, 65–86. New York: New Press.

Muñoz, José Esteban. 1999. *Disidentifications: Queers of Color and the Performance of Politics.* Minneapolis: University of Minnesota Press.

Nagy-Zekmi, Silvia, and Fernando Leiva, eds. 2005. *Democracy in Chile: The Legacy of September 11, 1973.* Brighton, UK: Sussex Academic.

Nelson, Alice A. 2002. *Political Bodies: Gender, History, and the Struggle for Narrative Power in Recent Chilean Literature.* Lewisburg, PA: Bucknell University Press.

Nichols, Bill. 1991. *Representing Reality: Issues and Concepts in Documentary.* Bloomington: Indiana University Press.

Nora, Pierre. 2001. *Rethinking France: Les lieux de mémoire.* Chicago: University of Chicago Press.

Núñez, Guillermo, ed. 1993. *Retrato hablado: Una retrospectiva.* Santiago: Museo de Arte Contemporáneo, Universidad de Chile.

O'Donnell, Guillermo. 1992. "Transitions, Continuities, and Paradoxes." In *Issues in Democratic Consolidation,* ed. Scott Mainwaring, Guillermo O'Donnell, and J. Samuel Valenzuela, 17–56. Notre Dame, IN: University of Notre Dame Press.

Olea, Raquel. 1993. "Textura del diálogo en la obra de Guillermo Núñez." In *Retrato hablado: Una retrospectiva,* ed. Guillermo Núñez, 63–66. Santiago: Museo de Arte Contemporáneo, Universidad de Chile.

Olea, Raquel, and Olga Grau, eds. 2001. *Volver a la memoria.* Santiago: Lom Ediciones.

Olick, Jeffrey K. 1999. "Collective Memory: The Two Cultures." *Sociological Theory* 17 (3): 333.

——, ed. 2003. *States of Memory: Continuities, Conflicts, and Transformations in National Retrospection.* Durham, NC: Duke University Press.

——. 2007. *The Politics of Regret: On Collective Memory and Historical Responsibility.* New York: Routledge.

Omi, Michael, and Howard Winant. 1994. *Racial Formation in the United States: From the 1960s to the 1990s.* New York: Routledge.

Ortega, Julio. 2000. *Caja de herramientas: Prácticas culturales para el nuevo siglo chileno.* Santiago: Lom Ediciones.

Oxhorn, Philip D., and Graciela Ducatenzeiler, eds. 1998. *What Kind of Democracy? What Kind of Market? Latin America in the Age of Neoliberalism.* University Park: Pennsylvania State University Press.

Paley, Julia. 2001. *Marketing Democracy: Power and Social Movements in Post-Dictatorship Chile.* Berkeley: University of California Press.

La Peña Cultural Center. "About Us: History and Mission." www.lapena.org/index.php?s=2 (accessed July 24, 2006).

Petras, James, and Fernando Ignacio Leiva. 1994. *Democracy and Poverty in Chile: The Limits to Electoral Politics.* Boulder: Westview.

Pick, Zuzana. 1993. *The New Latin American Cinema: A Continental Project.* Austin: University of Texas Press.

Pontecorvo, Gillo. 1966. *The Battle of Algiers.* Algiers: Casbah Films.

Portales, Felipe. 2000. *Chile: Una democracia tutelada.* Santiago: Editorial Sudamericana.

Pratt, Mary. 1999. "Overwriting Pinochet: Undoing the Culture of Fear in Chile." In *The Places of History: Regionalism Revisited in Latin America,* ed. Doris Sommer, 21–33. Durham, NC: Duke University Press.

Probyn, Elspeth. 1999. "Bloody Metaphors and Other Allegories of the Ordinary." In *Between Woman and Nation: Nationalisms, Transnational Feminisms, and the State,* ed. Caren Kaplan, Norma Alarcón, and Minoo Moallem, 47–62. Durham, NC: Duke University Press.

———. 2005. *Blush: Faces of Shame.* Minneapolis: University of Minnesota Press.

Quijano, Aníbal. 1997a. "The Colonial Nature of Power and Latin America's Cultural Experience." Paper presented at the International Sociological Association Regional Conference for Latin American, Colonia Tovar, Venezuela, July 7–8. In *Sociology in Latin America,* ed. Roberto Briceño-León, Heinz Rudolf Sonntag, and María Luz Morán, March 3, 1999. www.isa-sociology.org/reg/vol5.htm (accessed April 23, 2008).

———. 1997b. "Colonialidad del poder, cultura y conocimiento en América Latina." *Anuario Mariateguiano* 9 (9): 113–21.

Ranchod-Nilsson, Sita, and Mary Ann Tétreault, eds. 2000. *Women, States, and Nationalism: At Home in the Nation.* London: Routledge.

Rejali, Darius. 1994. *Torture and Modernity: Self, Society and State in Modern Iran.* Boulder, CO: Westview.

Renov, Michael. 2004. "Early Newsreel: The Construction of a Political Imaginary for the New Left." In *The Subject of Documentary,* ed. Michael Renov, 3–20. Minneapolis: University of Minnesota Press.

Retrato Hablado: Retrospectiva de la obra de Guillermo Núñez. 1993. Santiago: Museo de Arte Contemporáneo, Universidad de Chile. Exhibit catalog.

Rettig, Raúl (chair), Jaime Castillo Velasco, José Luis Cea Egaña, Mónica Jiménez de la Jara, Laura Novoa Vásquez, José Zalaquett Daher, Ricardo Martín Díaz, and Gonzalo Vial Correa. 1991. *The National Commission for Truth and Reconciliation Report.* Santiago, Chile.

Reyes, Andreani, Maria José, and María Francisca Juricic Cerda. 2000. *El si-no de la reconciliación: Representaciones sociales de la reconciliación nacional en los jóvenes.* Santiago: Fundación de Documentación y Archivo de la Vicaría de la Solidaridad.

Richard, Nelly. 1998. *Residuos y metáforas: Ensayos de crítica cultural sobre el Chile de la transición.* Santiago: Editorial Cuarto Propio.

———, ed. 2000. *Políticas y estéticas de la memoria.* Santiago: Editorial Cuarto Propio.

———. 2001 "Sitios de la memoria: Vaciamiento del recuerdo." *Revista de Crítica Cultural* 23 (November).

———, ed. 2004. *Arte y política desde 1960 en Chile.* Special issue, *Revista de crítica cultural* 29/30 (November).

Ríos Tobar, Marcela. 2003. "Feminism Is Socialism, Liberty and Much More: Second-Wave Chilean Feminism and Its Contentious Relationship with Socialism." *Journal of Women's History* 15 (3): 129–34.

Robben, Antonius C. G. M. 1995. "Seduction and Persuasion: The Politics of Truth and Emotion among Victims and Perpetrators of Violence." In *Fieldwork under Fire: Contemporary Studies of Violence and Survival,* ed. Carolyn Nordstrom and Antonius C. G. M, 81–103. Berkeley: University of California Press.

———. 1996. "Ethnographic Seduction, Transference, and Resistance in Dialogues about Terror and Violence in Argentina." *Ethos* 24 (1): 71–106.

———. 2000. "The Assault on Basic Trust: Disappearance, Protest, and Reburial in Argentina." In *Cultures under Siege: Collective Violence and Trauma*, ed. Antonius C. G. M. Robben and Marcelo M. Suárez-Orozco, 70–101. Cambridge: Cambridge University Press.

Robben, Antonius C. G. M, and Marcelo M. Suárez-Orozco. 2000. Introd. to *Cultures under Siege: Collective Violence and Trauma*, ed. Antonius C. G. M. Robben and Marcelo M. Suárez-Orozco. Cambridge: Cambridge University Press.

Rojas, Carmen. Circa 1981. *Recuerdos de una Mirista*. Independent publication, Santiago.

Rojas, María Teresa. 2000. "Reflexiones y creaciones: la memoria en el arte." In *Memoria para un nuevo siglo: Chile, miradas a la segunda mitad del siglo XX*, ed. Mario Garcés, Pedro Milos, Myriam Olguín, Julio Pinto, María Teresa Rojas, Miguel Larentis Urrutia, 297–301. Santiago: Lom Ediciones.

Rojas Mira, Claudia. 2001. "La tumba de los asesinados en los hornos de Lonquén." In *Volver a la memoria*, ed. Raquel Olea and Olga Grau. Santiago: Lom Ediciones.

Roniger, Luis, and Mario Sznajder. 1999. *The Legacy of Human-Rights Violations in the Southern Cone: Argentina, Chile, and Uruguay*. Oxford: Oxford University Press.

Said, Edward. 1999. "No Reconciliation Allowed." In *Letters of Transit: Reflections on Exile, Identity, Language and Loss*, ed. André Aciman, 87–114. New York: New Press.

Saldaña-Portillo, María Josefina. 2003. *The Revolutionary Imagination in the Americas and the Age of Development*. Durham, NC: Duke University Press.

Santa Cruz, Guadalupe. 1999. "Santiago fugaz: Memoria y territorio." *Revista de Crítica Cultural* 19 (November): 44–47.

Sassen, Saskia. 1998. *Globalization and Its Discontents: Essays on the New Mobility of People and Money*. New York: New Press.

Saunders, Rebecca, and Kamran Aghaie. 2005. "Introduction: Mourning and Memory." *Comparative Studies of South Asia, Africa and the Middle East* 25 (1): 16–29.

Scarry, Elaine. 1985. *The Body in Pain.* New York: Oxford University Press.

Schoenberg, Karl. 2000. *Levi's Children: Coming to Terms with Human Rights in the Global Marketplace.* New York: Atlantic Monthly.

Schwarzer, Mitchell. 1999. "Remembering the Holocaust and Its Aftershocks." In *Design Book Review: Architecture Design Urbanism Landscape,* 8–21. San Francisco: California College of Arts and Crafts.

Seidman, Steve. 1997. *Difference Troubles: Queering Social Theory and Sexual Politics.* Cambridge: Cambridge University Press.

———. 2000. "Relativizing Sociology: The Challenge of Cultural Studies." In *From Sociology to Cultural Studies: New Perspectives,* ed. Elizabeth Long 37–61. Oxford: Blackwell.

Shayne, July D. (2004). *Revolution Question: Feminisms in El Salvador, Chile and Cuba.* New Brunswick, NJ: Rutgers University Press.

Spillman, Lyn, ed. 2005. *Cultural Sociology.* Boston: Blackwell.

Stacey, Judith. 1996. *In the Name of the Family: Rethinking Family Values in the Postmodern Age.* Boston: Beacon.

Stephen, Lynn. 1994. *Hear My Testimony: María Teresa Tula, Human Rights Activist of El Salvador.* Boston: South End.

Stern, Steve J. 2001. "De la memoria suelta a la memoria emblemática: Hacia el recordar y el olvidar como proceso histórico (Chile, 1973–1998)." In *Memoria para un nuevo siglo: Chile, miradas a la segunda mitad del siglo XX,* ed. Mario Garcés, Pedro Milos, Myriam Olguín, Julio Pinto, María Teresa Rojas, and Miguel Larentis Urrutia. Santiago: Lom Ediciones.

———. 2004. *Remembering Pinochet's Chile: On the Eve of London 1998.* First book of *The Memory Box of Pinochet's Chile.* Durham, NC: Duke University Press.

———. 2009 (forthcoming). *Reckoning with Pinochet: The Memory Question in Democratic Chile, 1989–2006.* Third book of *The Memory Box of Pinochet's Chile.* Durham, NC: Duke University Press.

Stier, Oren Baruch. 2003. *Committed to Memory: Cultural Mediations of the Holocaust.* Amherst: University of Massachusetts Press.

Straker, Gill, Michaela Mendelsohn, Fathima Moosa, and Pam Tudin.

1992."Violent Political Contexts and the Emotional Concerns of Township Youth." *Child Development* 67 (1): 46–54.

Sturken, Marita. 1997. *Tangled Memories: The Vietnam War, the AIDS Epidemic, and the Politics of Remembering.* Berkeley: University of California Press.

Sturken, Marita, and Sarah Banet-Weiser. 2006. "Consumer Citizenship and the Making of National and Transnational Values." Panel at the American Studies Association meeting, Oakland, CA, October 13.

Taylor, Diana. 2003. *The Archive and the Repertoire: Performing Cultural Memory in the Americas.* Durham, NC: Duke University Press.

Valech, Sergio, María Luisa Sepúlveda, Miguel Luis Amunátegui, Luciano Fouillioux, José Antonio Gómez, Lucas Sierra, Álvaro Varela, and Elizabeth Lira. 2004. *The National Commission on Political Imprisonment and Torture Report. (The Valech Report).* Santiago, Chile.

Valenzuela, J. Samuel. 1995. "Orígenes y transformaciones del sistema de partidos en Chile." *Estudios Públicos* 58 (Fall): 5–77.

Valenzuela, Luisa. 1979. *Strange Things Happen Here.* New York: Harcourt.

Varas, José Miguel. 2001. "¡No nos torturen más!" *Rocinante: arte, cultura, sociedad* 4, no. 28 (February): 28–29.

Vergara, Pilar. 1994. "Market Economy, Social Welfare, and Democratic Consolidation in Chile." In *Democracy, Markets and Structural Reform in Latin America: Argentina, Bolivia, Brazil, Chile, and Mexico,* ed. William C. Smith, Carlos H. Acuña, and Eduardo A. Gamarra, 237–58. New Brunswick, NJ: Transaction.

Vidal, Hernán. 1979. "The Politics of the Body: The Chilean Junta and the Anti-Fascist Struggle." *Social Text* 2 (Summer): 104–19.

Vidaldi, Anna. 1996. "Political Identity, Identification and Transmission of Trauma." *New Formations: A Journal of Culture/Theory/Politics.* Special issue, *Cultural Memory,* no. 30 (Winter): 33–45.

Villalobos-Ruminott, Sergio. 2000. "Critical Thought in Post-Dictatorship." *Journal of Latin American Cultural Studies* 9 (3): 229–34.

Volkan, Vamik D., and Norman Itzkowitz. 2000. "Modern Greek and Turkish Identities and the Psychodynamics of Greek-Turkish Relations." In *Cultures under Siege: Collective Violence and Trauma*, ed. Antonius C. G. M. Robben and Marcelo M. Suárez-Orozco. Cambridge: Cambridge University Press.

Wagner-Pacifici, Robin, and Barry Schwartz. 2002. "The Vietnam Veterans Memorial: Commemorating a Difficult Past." In *Cultural Sociology*, ed. Lyn Spillman, 210–20. Malden, MA: Blackwell.

Walker, Janet. 2003. *Trauma Cinema: Documenting Incest and the Holocaust.* Berkeley: University of California Press.

Walkowitz, Daniel J., and Knauer, Lisa Maya, eds. 2004. *Memory and the Impact of Political Transformation in Public Space.* Durham, NC: Duke University Press.

Wall, Catharine E. 2003. "Bilingualism and Identity in Julia Alvarez's poem 'Bilingual Sestina.'" *MELUS* 28 (4): 125–45.

Weber, Max. 1978. *Economy and Society: An Outline of Interpretive Sociology.* 2 vols. Berkeley: University of California Press.

Weinstein, Eugenia, and Elizabeth Lira. 1987. "La Tortura." In *Trauma, duelo y reparación: Una experiencia de trabajo psicosocial en Chile*, ed. Eugenia Weinstein, et al. 33–60. Santiago: Fasic Editorial.

Westphal, Germán F. 2003. "The *Esmeralda* Ship: The Chilean Navy's Torture Chamber." International Committee against Impunity in Chile, www.chile-esmeralda.com (accessed November 18, 2007).

Wilde, Alexander. 1999. "Irruptions of Memory: Expressive Politics in Chile's Transition to Democracy." *Journal of Latin American Studies* 31 (2): 471–500.

Williams, Linda. 1995. "Film Bodies: Gender, Genre, Excess." In *Film Genre Reader II*, ed. Barry Grant. Austin: University of Texas Press.

Williams, Raymond. 1977. *Marxism and Literature.* Oxford: Oxford University Press.

Winn, Peter. 1989. *Weavers of the Revolution: The Yarur Workers and Chile's Road to Socialism.* New York: Oxford University Press.

———, ed. 2004. *Victims of the Chilean Miracle: Workers and Neoliberalism in the Pinochet Era, 1973–2002.* Durham, NC: Duke University Press.

Yoneyama, Lisa. 1999. *Hiroshima: Traces, Time, Space and the Dialectics of Memory.* Berkeley: University of California Press.

Youdelman, Jeffrey. 1988. "Narration, Invention, and History." In *New Challenges for Documentary*, ed. Alan Rosenthal, 397–408. Berkeley: University of California Press.

Young, James E. 1993. *The Texture of Memory: Holocaust Memorials and Meaning*. New Haven: Yale University Press.

Yúdice, George. 2003. *The Expediency of Culture: Uses of Culture in the Global Era*. Durham, NC: Duke University Press.

Zelizer, Barbie. 1998. *Remembering to Forget: Holocaust Memory through the Camera's Eye*. Chicago: University of Chicago Press.

———. 2001a. "Introduction: On Visualizing the Holocaust." In *Visual Culture and the Holocaust*, 1–12. New Brunswick, NJ: Rutgers University Press.

———, ed. 2001b. *Visual Culture and the Holocaust*. New Brunswick, NJ: Rutgers University Press.

Zerubavel, Eviatar. 2006. *The Elephant in the Room: Silence and Denial in Everyday Life*. Oxford: Oxford University Press.

INDEX

Page numbers in *italics* refer to figures.

Compositor: Integrated Composition Systems
Indexer: J. Naomi Linzer Indexing Services
Text: 10/15 Janson
Display: Janson
Printer/Binder: Thomson-Shore, Inc.